D1327311

NEW DIRECTIONS FOR TEACHING AND LEARNING

Robert J. Menges, *Northwestern University*
EDITOR-IN-CHIEF

Marilla D. Svinicki, *University of Texas, Austin*
ASSOCIATE EDITOR

# Disciplinary Differences in Teaching and Learning: Implications for Practice

Nira Hativa
*Tel Aviv Univeristy*

Michele Marincovich
*Stanford University*

EDITORS

Number 64, Winter 1995

JOSSEY-BASS PUBLISHERS
San Francisco

Disciplinary Differences in Teaching and Learning: Implications for Practice
Nira Hativa, Michele Marincovich (eds.)
New Directions for Teaching and Learning, no. 64
Robert J. Menges, Editor-in-Chief
Marilla D. Svinicki, Associate Editor

Microfilm copies of issues and articles are available in 16mm and 35mm, as well as microfiche in 105mm, through University Microfilms Inc., 300 North Zeeb Road, Ann Arbor, Michigan 48106-1346.

ISSN 0271-0633     ISBN 0-7879-9909-1     April 8, 1996

NEW DIRECTIONS FOR TEACHING AND LEARNING is part of The Jossey-Bass Higher and Adult Education Series and is published quarterly by Jossey-Bass Inc., Publishers, 350 Sansome Street, San Francisco, California 94104-1342. Second-class postage paid at San Francisco, California, and at additional mailing offices. POSTMASTER: Send address changes to New Directions for Teaching and Learning, Jossey-Bass Inc., Publishers, 350 Sansome Street, San Francisco, California 94104-1342.

SUBSCRIPTIONS for 1995 cost $48.00 for individuals and $64.00 for institutions, agencies, and libraries.

EDITORIAL CORRESPONDENCE should be sent to the editor-in-chief, Robert J. Menges, Northwestern University, Center for the Teaching Professions, 2115 North Campus Drive, Evanston, Illinois 60208-2610.

Cover photograph by Richard Blair/Color & Light © 1990.

Manufactured in the United States of America on Lyons Falls Pathfinder Tradebook. This paper is acid-free and 100 percent totally chlorine-free.

# CONTENTS

*About This Publication.* Since 1980, *New Directions for Teaching and Learning (NDTL)* has brought a unique blend of theory, research, and practice to leaders in postsecondary education. *NDTL* sourcebooks strive not only for solid substance but also for timeliness, compactness, and accessibility.

The series has four goals: to inform readers about current and future directions in teaching and learning in postsecondary education, to illuminate the context that shapes these new directions, to illustrate these new directions through examples from real settings, and to propose ways in which these new directions can be incorporated into still other settings.

This publication reflects our view that teaching deserves respect as a high form of scholarship. We believe that significant scholarship is conducted not only by researchers who report results of empirical investigations but also by practitioners who share disciplined reflections about teaching. Contributors to *NDTL* approach questions of teaching and learning as seriously as they approach substantive questions in their own disciplines, and they deal not only with pedagogical issues but also with the intellectual and social context in which these issues arise. Authors deal on the one hand with theory and research and on the other with practice, and they translate from research and theory to practice and back again.

*About This Volume.* This volume of *New Directions for Teaching and Learning* offers research-based essays about the pervasive influence of academic disciplines on faculty beliefs, on our teaching, and on the learning of our students. Students do not intuitively grasp the disciplinary perspectives that seem so obvious to faculty. These chapters suggest ways to enhance students' experiences through better knowledge of disciplinary differences and through more thorough understanding of the learning process.

Robert J. Menges, *Editor-in-Chief*
Marilla D. Svinicki, *Associate Editor*

ROBERT J. MENGES, *editor-in-chief, is professor of education and social policy at Northwestern University, and senior researcher, National Center on Post-secondary Teaching, Learning, and Assessment.*

MARILLA D. SVINICKI, *associate editor, is director of the Center for Teaching Effectiveness, University of Texas at Austin.*

# EDITORS' NOTES

Those who work in higher education soon learn the importance of the disciplinary context of almost all academic endeavor; those who try to go beyond that context by doing interdisciplinary studies are probably most aware of the power of the disciplines. In spite of their practical and pervasive influence, however, the disciplines themselves have been subjected to relatively little systematic study, especially in their effect on the quality of teaching and learning in higher education. It is the purpose of this volume to provide new summaries of important studies on disciplinary differences and to point out promising directions for further research.

Our starting point, in almost every case, is the work of Anthony Biglan (1973). Over twenty years ago, he established an insightful and durable model of disciplinary differences; using three dimensions, he sorted thirty-six fields in colleges and universities into eight (2 × 2 × 2) cells, reflecting similarities and differences in the subject matter they represented. These dimensions are the degree of consensus or paradigm development ("hard" versus "soft"), the extent of practical application ("applied" versus "pure"), and the presence or absence of involvement with living objects or organisms ("life" versus "nonlife"). Biglan assumed that academic areas that belong to different cells require different methods for teaching and learning. Although a reasonable number of studies have validated Biglan's model, and some of those have indeed identified similarities and differences in the teaching and learning of subject areas belonging to the different cells, the intervening years have not seen a steady growth in either the practical or the scholarly influence of Biglan's insights.

Most student evaluations of teaching, for example, use the same form to evaluate faculty in all disciplines, and the results of ratings are interpreted for tenure and promotion decisions in the same general manner across departments. Similarly, most centers for teaching improvement employ the same instructional consultant to work with faculty in very different departments as if teaching patterns, goals, and needs are practically the same regardless of discipline. This notion reflects the once influential approach of the University of Massachusetts Clinic to Improve University Teaching, which assumed that it was sufficient for a consultant to have expertise in effective teaching methods generally and that these would apply across disciplines.

Recent years have brought some change, in large part thanks to Lee S. Shulman (1986, 1987) and the researchers he has trained. There has been a growing recognition of the need to take into consideration disciplinary differences in doing research on teaching as well as in evaluating and making decisions related to faculty on the basis of their student evaluations. There is also a growing recognition of the differences in student needs in learning different disciplines. As a response, a few centers for university/college teaching employ specialized consultants, each developing expertise in a particular group of disciplines.

Still, the issues related to disciplinary differences continue to be vaguely defined and underexplored. Of the literally thousands of studies of teaching, learning, and teacher evaluation in higher education, very few have examined disciplinary differences. To improve instruction and to interpret student ratings appropriately across disciplines, we need to increase our knowledge and understanding of the causes and consequences of disciplinary differences in teaching and learning. We need to know the structure and organization of disciplines, the culture and environment in which teaching takes place, and the differences among faculty and students across disciplines regarding their attitudes toward instruction, their goals, beliefs, values, philosophies, and orientations. University faculty need to know more about good teaching approaches in their particular discipline, and about the problems and difficulties of their students in learning their particular subject matter. Faculty developers need to understand these issues in order to improve instruction in particular domain areas, and administrators need to recognize differences in students' evaluations of their instructors in different disciplines in order to make appropriate decisions.

To address these issues, the volume contains eleven chapters divided into three parts. Part One deals with differences in the types of knowledge that university faculty prize in their discipline and emphasize in their teaching. Janet G. Donald examines validation processes in five academic disciplines, and Nira Hativa looks at the differences between a matched pair of pure and applied academic fields in the types of knowledge that are emphasized in classroom lectures.

Part Two concentrates on faculty and teaching. Harry G. Murray and Robert D. Renaud examine disciplinary differences in classroom teaching behaviors and their relationship to student ratings of instruction. Building on the recent work of Gerald Gillmore (1994), Jennifer Franklin and Michael Theall add a variable—"student perceptions of the value of time spent preparing for class"—to the list of variables that affect student ratings of their instructors and show how the "time-valued ratio," as well as several other variables that are commonly described as sources of systematic variation in ratings of overall instructor effectiveness, vary by course discipline. John C. Smart and Corinna A. Ethington concentrate on attitudes of over four thousand faculty from twenty-eight academic disciplines toward the most important goals for undergraduate instruction. These attitudes are examined for disciplinary differences sorted on the basis of two criteria: the Biglan model and the Carnegie classification for colleges and universities. John M. Braxton also uses a set of Biglan categories—the soft versus hard—to examine faculty attitudes toward the reform of undergraduate education and concludes that faculty in soft disciplines have an affinity for educational reform. They are natural allies for those who are undertaking change and improvement in the undergraduate curriculum. Lisa Firing Lenze uses Shulman's concept of pedagogical content knowledge and the work of his one-time student, Pamela L. Grossman, to examine differences between the knowledge new faculty in a social science discipline and a humanities discipline bring to teaching. Susan S. Stodolsky and Pamela L. Grossman summarize research on the ways in which subject matter (in five disciplinary areas) shapes high school teachers' work and beliefs and explore the implications of this research for instruction in higher education.

Part Three addresses students and their learning. William E. Cashin and Ronald G. Downey use the huge data base of the IDEA (Instructional Development and Effectiveness Assessment) system of student evaluations of teaching to examine eight disciplines (one from each of Biglan's cells) to discover what the faculty in these eight fields emphasize in their teaching, what students in these fields report that they have learned, and what these students say about the teaching methods used. Noel Entwistle and Hilary Tait summarize research on students from a variety of English universities regarding students' styles of learning and study approaches. They then discuss the relationships between these styles and approaches and students' perceptions of the learning environment created, often unconsciously, by faculty and their departments. Verena H. Menec and Raymond P. Perry present a therapeutic technique to modify potentially maladaptive perceptions of students regarding what it takes to succeed in a discipline.

Finally, in concluding remarks, Michele Marincovich explores some of the unspoken assumptions reflected in these chapters, points out further lines of investigation, and wonders if our study of disciplines may eventually temper rather than exacerbate the sharpness of the differences.

In its coverage of both teaching and learning, both higher education in its own right and in its relationship to secondary education, we hope this volume appeals to the faculty, teaching assistants, and lecturers who teach in our colleges and universities; to those who make decisions about the policy and organization of higher education, whether they are in our postsecondary institutions or in government and foundations; and to those who work with students in learning centers and student affairs. Clearly, few aspects of academia are more compelling and enduring than the disciplines. Perhaps the only more important aspect is to continue to subject the disciplines themselves to study.

Nira Hativa
Michele Marincovich

## References

Biglan, A. "The Characteristics of Subject Matter in Different Academic Areas." *Journal of Applied Psychology,* 1973, *57* (3), 195–203.

Gillmore, G. "The Effects of Course Demands and Grading Leniency on Student Ratings of Instruction." Paper presented at the annual meeting of the American Educational Research Association, Atlanta, April 1994.

Shulman, L. S. "Those Who Understand: Knowledge Growth in Teaching." *Educational Researcher,* 1986, *15* (2) 4–14.

Shulman, L. S. "Knowledge and Teaching: Foundations of the New Reform." *Harvard Educational Review,* 1987, *57,* 1–22.

*Nira Hativa is professor in the School of Education and faculty developer in the Natural Science and Engineering Departments at Tel Aviv University. In 1994–95 she was a visiting professor in the Department of Physics at Stanford University under a grant from the Peter and Helen Bing Fund for Teaching at Stanford.*

*Michele Marincovich is director of the Center for Teaching and Learning at Stanford University.*

# PART ONE

Differences Among Disciplines in the Structure of Knowledge (What Is Being Taught)

*Validation processes and truth criteria employed in a discipline*
*define the discipline, govern knowledge production and dissemination*
*in the discipline, and suggest ways of improving instruction.*

# Disciplinary Differences in Knowledge Validation

*Janet G. Donald*

Scholarly disciplines have been described as communities, networks, or domains with defining modes of enquiry and conceptual structures (King and Brownell, 1966). A discipline is expected to meet certain criteria, for example, to possess a specialized body of knowledge or theory with a reasonably logical taxonomy so that gaps in accepted knowledge can be recognized (Dressel and Mayhew, 1974). A discipline is also expected to have techniques for theory testing and revision and a sense of sequence, which enables scholars to predict where they should look next. Disciplines are defined epistemologically by their distinctive sets of concepts, the logical structure of propositions, the truth criteria by which propositions are assessed, and the methodology employed to produce the propositions (Donald, 1986; Hirst, 1974; Toulmin, 1972). Thus, the method by which knowledge is arrived at in a discipline, its process of knowledge validation, and the truth criteria employed in that process are essential to the definition of the discipline.

Disciplines meet these expectations to varying degrees. The physical sciences best meet these expectations and are described as *well structured* or *paradigmatic* (Donald, 1987; Frederiksen, 1984). They are also known as *hard* or *restricted*, because the field of phenomena is limited, methods are tightly defined, and research is highly replicable (Becher, 1989; Pantin, 1968). To the extent that a discipline does not meet these criteria, it is considered to be *soft, unrestricted,* or *less well structured;* content and method are more idiosyncratic (Becher, 1989;

This chapter is based on research funded by the Social Sciences and Humanities Research Council of Canada, the Québec Fonds pour la Formation de Chercheurs et l'Aide à la Recherche, and the Academic Development Fund of Monash University in Clayton, Australia.

Biglan, 1973; Frederiksen, 1984). In less well-structured disciplines, as in the social sciences and humanities, complexity is regarded as a legitimate aspect of knowledge; *unrestricted* refers to the fact that the field of phenomena is relatively unlimited. The least well-structured areas of study are more often referred to as fields of study, characterized by being ill-defined in their parameters and lacking a logical structure of knowledge and a generally accepted methodology (Dressel and Mayhew, 1974). Applied areas of study, such as engineering and education, are sometimes described as fields because the phenomena they study are relatively unrestricted and the methods are diverse.

What is not known is the extent to which methods of validation vary across disciplines. This is not an easy question to answer, as different models and terms have been used to describe the method of validation processes in different disciplines. For example, in the humanities, the methods most commonly referred to are hermeneutics and critical thinking. In the sciences, problem solving and the scientific method are most frequently used to describe validation processes. To understand how distinctive the methods of validation are posited to be in different disciplines, it is first necessary to examine these models and their use in particular disciplines.

## Models Used to Describe the Process of Knowledge Validation

The earliest model to describe the process of knowledge validation was that of *hermeneutics,* used to analyze biblical text. Hermeneutics, or interpretation, is the construction of textual meaning, which elucidates the connotations that text explicitly or implicitly represents (Hirsch, 1967). This is accomplished through a dialectic between understanding, which is directed toward the intentional unity of discourse, and explanation, which is more directed toward the analytic structure of a text (Ricoeur, 1976). Hermeneutics is viewed in terms of a circle in which guess and validation are related as subjective and objective approaches to the text. The first act of understanding is a guess as to the meaning of the text. The transition from guessing to explanation is secured by an investigation of the specific object of guessing. One begins by assuming that the text is coherent, and one then develops a framework of explanation which is tested by the facts it generates. The method is thus a process of hypothesizing and then searching for corroborating evidence in the text. Although the hermeneutic approach is espoused most frequently in the humanities, discourse analysis as currently utilized in the social sciences owes much to hermeneutics.

A model more generally applied across disciplines, *critical thinking,* developed out of the Socratic tradition of disciplined inquiry. Usually defined as a reasoned or questioning approach in which one examines assumptions and seeks evidence (Donald, 1985), researchers suggest that critical thinking includes components of logic, problem solving, and Piagetian formal operations (Meyers, 1986; Sternberg, 1985). Different disciplines also appear to focus on different aspects of the critical thinking process—inferential processes in physics compared with testing assumptions in English (Donald, 1985; Meyers, 1986).

In comparison to critical thinking, *problem solving* is described more specifically as a set of steps consisting of formulating or representing a problem, selecting the relations pertinent to solving the problem, doing the necessary calculations, and verifying the logic used to see if the final answer makes sense (Reif, Larkin, and Brackett, 1976). Thus, problem solving includes not only critical thinking but also processes of implementation or testing; the difference between critical thinking and problem solving may be seen as analogous to that of comprehending versus doing.

The *scientific method* is a model that consists of universal standards for knowledge claims, common ownership of information, disinterestedness or integrity in gathering and interpreting data, and organized skepticism (Krathwohl, 1985). Popper (1959) claimed that skepticism, the active attempt to disconfirm knowledge claims, is how science proceeds, implying deduction; but Krathwohl argues that we tend to think inductively, as if knowledge had some certainty and is tested for generality and strength under varying circumstances. Science is defined by the objective nature of its methods, the replicability of findings, the insistence on empirical demonstrations, and its self-correcting nature; that is, findings are held as tentative until they are replaced by better-established knowledge claims.

Krathwohl points out that the social sciences tend to interpret these characteristics somewhat differently from the physical sciences. For example, in the physical sciences, objectivity is based on the assumption that a phenomenon exists in the real world and hence is observable or verifiable by scientific methods. In contrast, in the social sciences one attempts to establish interrater reliability, where phenomena observed by one researcher are seen or perceived in the same way by another. An element of perception or interpretation enters into the process.

## Differences Across Disciplines in Validation Processes

Models describing validation processes were developed with reference to one or a limited number of domains or subject-matter areas and so have employed different scholarly languages to describe the phenomenon of knowledge validation. Hermeneutics was developed to study biblical text and has been used primarily in the study of literature, but more recently it has been utilized in the social sciences. Critical thinking is utilized more broadly in the humanities, particularly philosophy. Problem solving is the term of choice in the physical sciences, although the scientific method is also used to describe thinking in the physical and social sciences. Because the humanistic disciplines are concerned with phenomena that do not have immediate referents, one author has suggested that humanistic truth involves something other than logical or scientific validity (Broudy, 1977). In contrast to the humanists, social scientists have been trained to discern and formulate patterns which can be expressed in general terms (Rosenberg, 1979). They can therefore create models which can be tested and verified, similar to the problem-solving process in the physical sciences.

In an attempt to relate the truth strategies used in different disciplines, Thompson, Hawkes, and Avery (1969) compared disciplines by the extent to which they rely on experience and by how explicit and systematic their logical structure or code of reasoning is. The sciences are described as combining high reliance on experience with systematic theorizing, while the humanities are said to rely on experience but not on a specific code of reasoning. Mathematics and logic, on the other hand, are independent of experience but highly structured and systematic. According to Thompson, Hawkes, and Avery, disciplines relying on both experience and systematic theorizing have a double-checking procedure for eliminating error, and can therefore claim a high degree of validity. In disciplines using only experience, however, argument and criticism coupled with consistency over time determine the validity of experience.

The truth criteria employed to judge validity may vary across disciplines. Although consistency appears to be an important criterion in all disciplines, in the humanities it is consistency over time and across people, while in the social sciences consistency takes the form of reliability over a series of observations. Precision or accuracy could be considered a direct measure of structure or codification, but in less well-structured or more complex domains the coherence of the argument or the completeness or comprehensiveness of the theory is more important.

In summary, using the Biglan (1973) categories, professors from the physical sciences could be expected to test experience against systematic theorizing. Social scientists could be expected to follow the same pattern to some degree, but not to display the same degree of structure or specificity that is expected of natural scientists. Humanities professors would not be in a position to test experience against systematic theory, but they would be interested in the test of time as a means of validating experience.

## A Study of Knowledge Validation Processes

In order to test hypotheses about the validation processes used in different disciplines, forty professors, nominated by their colleagues at four English language research universities as expert teachers and researchers in their disciplines, were interviewed to determine how they validate knowledge in their disciplines. The professors were selected from five representative areas: physics, engineering, psychology, education, and English literature, to yield a sample of eight experts in each disciplinary area. According to the Biglan (1973) multidimensional scaling of disciplines in universities and colleges along dimensions of hard-soft and pure-applied, physics represents hard/pure; engineering, hard/applied; psychology, intermediate hard/pure (considered to be soft in the Biglan university sample but hard in the college sample and hard in the social sciences); education, soft/applied; and English literature, soft/pure. The professors were interviewed individually in structured but open interviews during the period 1986–1990; they were asked how they validated knowledge in their field of study and what they considered to be the most important truth criteria for validation. A report of the interview was sent to each professor, to be edited as an accurate representation of the professor's views.

A similarity grouping procedure was used on the important phrases excerpted from the reports to produce the processes used to validate knowledge. To do this, an analysis of all important phrases about validation and truth criteria was first done in a subset of reports to establish groupings of words and phrases which were most alike. The phrases were checked against individual reports to ensure that the group in which they had been placed was consistent with the meaning in the individual reports. Responses to the questions on validation and truth criteria were then excerpted in their entirety from the reports in the study. Important phrases from the reports were placed in the groups which had been developed in the study of the subset of reports. Each placement of a phrase in a group or category was cross-checked for reliability with the study of the subset, and then an independent grouping was done by a research assistant to ensure interrater reliability. More detailed methodology is described by Donald (1990).

## Validation Processes Favored in Different Disciplines

In contrast to the literature on models of validation processes, which suggests that professors would use terms such as "critical thinking" or "problem solving," the professors in the study were much more specific and concrete in their responses. The validation process mentioned most frequently was the use of empirical evidence, which included experiment, reproducibility, or performance, to test the truth of a phenomenon; 58 percent of the professors mentioned it (Table 1.1). Professors talked about judging how good the data are in supporting the hypothesis, about physical evidence, or about getting qualitative and quantitative agreement with observation and experiment. "Does it work?" was another way this was phrased, or whether analysis produces an explanation which fits the data. We could expect that physical science professors (from physics and engineering) would be most likely to mention the use of empirical evidence as a validation process, but as many psychologists (88 percent) emphasized using empirical evidence, and three-quarters of the educators also mentioned the use of empirical evidence. Although only half the professors of English literature put emphasis on the use of empirical evidence, differences between hard (physics, engineering, psychology) and soft (education, English literature) disciplines were not significant.

A relatively small proportion of professors (23 percent), all in the pure disciplines, mentioned the use of conflicting evidence, counterexamples, or alternative explanations, that is, the use of deductive logic to test for truth. Only in psychology did a majority of the professors (63 percent) note the importance of deductive logic methodologically. Because the use of conflicting evidence requires deductive thinking from a clearly postulated model, the lack

### Table 1.1.  Validation Processes, Criteria, and Factors Named by Professors (*n* = 40)

|  | Physics | Engineering | Psychology | Education | English Literature | Total |
|---|---|---|---|---|---|---|
| *Processes* | | | | | | |
| Use of empirical evidence, reproducibility, performance | 7 | 7 | 7 | 6 | 4 | 31 |
| Use of conflicting evidence, counterexamples, alternative explanations | 2 | 0 | 5 | 0 | 2 | 9 |
| Peer review, credibility, acceptability, plausibility | 3 | 1 | 2 | 3 | 4 | 13 |
| *Criteria* | | | | | | |
| Consistency, correspondence, reliability, uncertainty | 6 | 7 | 5 | 5 | 5 | 28 |
| Precision, accuracy, specificity | 5 | 3 | 3 | 2 | 5 | 18 |
| Coherence, internal consistency, parts tested against whole | 2 | 4 | 7 | 4 | 3 | 20 |
| *Factors* | | | | | | |
| Conceptual framework, model, design, comprehensiveness | 2 | 5 | 4 | 2 | 0 | 13 |
| Appropriate method, technique, procedure | 0 | 2 | 2 | 3 | 0 | 7 |
| Innovation, insight, important question; influences others | 1 | 0 | 1 | 1 | 3 | 6 |

of reference in applied areas could be expected, since applied disciplines must go beyond restricted, hence clearly postulated, models. One could suppose that hard or well-structured disciplines would be more likely to use such a strategy, and therefore that there would be a downward trend from physics to psychology to English literature professors, but this was not so. The low overall proportion suggests little academic accord with Popper's conviction (1959) that a belief is rationally grounded and respectable only if it has been submitted to a crucial experiment designed to falsify it and has succeeded in passing that test. At one time it was assumed (see Skinner, 1985) that Popper's test of falsification had become part of the scientist's code, but validation processes that rely upon empirical evidence had much wider acceptance among our experts than a test for falsification, confirming Krathwohl's argument (1985) for an inductive process of testing for generality.

The third kind of validation process, acceptance by an external authority, either through peer review or in terms of credibility or plausibility, was mentioned by approximately one-third of the experts distributed across the disciplines that were investigated. Half the English literature professors suggested its use for validation purposes, while engineers (13 percent) were least likely to mention its use. The results suggest that in English literature, reliance on empirical evidence is balanced by reliance on peer judgment.

These findings imply differences between disciplines in kinds of validation processes, but the only significant difference was between pure and applied disciplines in the use of conflicting evidence. If adherence to validation processes in general is a criterion of a hard discipline, psychology met the criterion more often (fourteen attributions) than physics (twelve), and English literature (ten) met the criterion more frequently than education (nine) or engineering (eight). There appears to be an interaction between hard and soft, pure and applied disciplines in the number of references to validation processes used, with members of pure disciplines giving greater recognition to validation processes.

## Validation Criteria Named in Different Disciplines

The criterion most mentioned by professors (70 percent) was consistency with the external world, which included references to correspondence, reliability, and degree of uncertainty. This criterion coincides theoretically with the validation process of using empirical evidence. "Consistency" was used to refer to reliability over time, situations, or persons, and thus proof by means of replicability, objectivity, or agreement. Some professors held that external and internal consistency were interdependent. In keeping with the ways in which the professors illustrated what consistency meant to them, however, consistency is used here to mean external consistency, and coherence is used to mean internal consistency.

Professors described consistency in terms of a proposition fitting in with preexisting knowledge or with what has been accepted before, as reliability across cases, or as measurement within an acceptable range. An engineering professor described it in these words: "Consistency implies that I have done three rather similar experiments; there are differences between the results but they seem to have a trend about them that is comprehensible." An English professor described consistency as the extent to which an interpretation of a play seems consonant with an interpretation of another play. Consistency therefore involves the idea of matching a conceptualization in the real world, or getting the same results from a series of cases or experiments. Physics professors (75 percent) and engineering professors (88 percent) named consistency as a criterion more frequently, with equal percentages of psychology, education, and English literature professors (63 percent) mentioning it.

Precision, accuracy, or specificity was chosen by 45 percent of the experts as a criterion of validity. Some professors said that precision was not a criterion of validity but was assumed in their field; one psychology professor stated that it was used as a preliminary screening device. In physics, several professors stated that no result is absolutely accurate; there is always some uncertainty. An engineering professor described the criterion in terms of encouraging students to have a concept of orders of magnitude, so that they could estimate within what range an answer should lie. The criterion was used most frequently by physics and English literature professors (63 percent). English professors sought accuracy in terms of relating textual detail or in whether text was historically sound. Thus the supposition that precision is used more frequently in hard disciplines as a criterion was not borne out.

Coherence or internal consistency was considered important to one half the professors, most prominently among psychologists (88 percent), while half the engineers and educators noted its importance. Among physicists, two used the term "internal consistency"; several pointed out that they would not use the term "coherence" as a criterion of validity because of its specific meaning in wave theory. A psychology professor spoke of building a computer program to model an explanation and discovering only by attempting to build an explicit model that it was radically incomplete and incoherent. An English professor considered coherence the most important criterion, stating that no interpretation of a play is entirely coherent, that is, takes into account every fact about a play, but the ones that take into consideration most of the facts about the play are the ones which are most coherent and therefore most answerable to the criterion of verification. Complexity limits the degree of coherence that can be expected.

## Other Validation Factors Reported in Different Disciplines

In addition to processes used to validate knowledge and criteria for judging it, the professors named other important factors guiding their process of validation.

Several professors, primarily in engineering and psychology, stated that an important part of validating their work was the development of a conceptual framework, testing a model, or building a design. They also spoke of the importance of a unified or comprehensive conception. One psychology professor spoke of coping with all the facts, being able to handle all the data in a comprehensive manner; another talked about telling a story which accommodates the largest proportion of the data. An engineering professor talked about a valid design as one that will work as a structure of a system, and a physicist used the following language: "most importantly, that you should have a model which qualitatively accounts for the phenomenon that you see, then [sic] which accounts for it quantitatively." Although these comments are close in meaning to the criterion of coherence, they go beyond it to a developed conception or design or model and closely approximate Thompson, Hawkes, and Avery's (1969) description of truth strategies in the sciences.

Conjunct with having an adequate framework or model is the attention paid by seven professors in engineering, psychology, and education to having an appropriate method, technique, or procedure. Professors spoke of the importance of looking at how technically good a piece of research is or evaluating a method for its appropriateness or a procedure for its validity. Innovation, insight, or the importance of the question being asked was more frequently noted by professors of English literature. A physicist and an educator both pointed to the need for addressing an important problem or question.

This was the most general approach taken to validation and concerned not only construct validity but also leadership in the field.

## Conclusions from the Study

More cohesion was found across disciplines than might have been expected, suggesting that there are common meeting grounds. The similarity most evident was in the widespread use of consistency as a criterion. The only significant difference was between pure and applied disciplines in the use of conflicting evidence. If we return to the models suggested by individual disciplines to describe the process of knowledge validation, we might expect the English literature professors to be in substantial agreement with the use of coherence as a criterion, since it most closely coincides with the hermeneutic process, a search for coherence. However, less than half the English professors made reference to coherence as a criterion, some explaining that textual complexity renders coherence of limited value as a criterion. Hermeneutics may be a useful method in theory, but in practice it appears that English professors encounter complexity or divergence more frequently than coherence. On the other hand, three-quarters of the psychologists noted the importance of coherence, which is consistent with the increased use of hermeneutics as discourse analysis in the social sciences.

The closest validation process to critical thinking would be the use of conflicting evidence, suggested only in pure disciplines and more frequently by psychology professors, although the use of empirical evidence, also part of the definition of critical thinking, was supported by all groups of scholars. The broad definition of critical thinking as a reasoned or questioning approach may render it less useful as a model of validation. Problem solving, on the other hand, has much in common with the most frequently mentioned process, the use of empirical evidence, and the most frequently mentioned criterion, consistency or correspondence. Krathwohl's definition of the scientific method as inductive is a much better match for the results of this study than is Popper's more narrow definition of the scientific method as deductive. Pure disciplines rather than hard disciplines appear to have the most rigorous verification procedures. Evidently, further study of the use of validation processes across disciplines is needed to test the appropriateness of the models to describe methods used to produce knowledge in different disciplines.

## Implications for Instruction

Although the professors did not explicitly link validation processes in their disciplines to the process of instruction in their courses, implications can be derived for the classroom. In science courses, professors commented about judging how good the data are in supporting the hypothesis, about physical evidence, or about getting qualitative and quantitative agreement with observation and experiment confirmed. These comments imply the importance of instruction that develops students' validation processes, such as problem solving and graphic representation. Psychology professors talked of developing students' capabilities through a series of courses which focus on different methods (Donald, 1994). In education, case studies are seen as important instructional methods to aid students in making complex situations coherent. English literature professors paid attention to the analysis of text to determine the underlying assumptions, consistent with the hermeneutic path, and they were concerned with the development of argument in their courses.

The relative lack of agreement within and across disciplines about how knowledge is validated—with the exception of the use of empirical evidence—suggests a problem for professors in the classroom. Students interpret the learning task as professors describe it. If professors themselves are not clear about how knowledge is validated, it may be well beyond possibility that students will receive adequate instruction in how to test and validate their own knowledge. Overall, diverse instructional methods were suggested by the professors that could be used to develop the ability to validate knowledge. Although lecturing played an important part in modeling validation methods, problem-solving groups and assignments—including open-ended projects, the analysis of cases or situations, workshops, and tutorials—also played prominent roles. In the professors' views, instruction that involves students in analyzing, hypothesizing, describing, and testing was essential for developing students' thinking processes. Most important, all faculty need to explicitly communicate the methods used in their discipline to students. As one psychology professor noted, it is the arguments or inferences in a discipline that must be learned. The findings of this study suggest that work is needed within the disciplines to provide students with clear expectations about what is important to learn and, more specifically, that they are expected to think and to validate their work. This will require emphasizing the structure of learning, orienting students to the challenges that postsecondary education provides.

## References

Becher, T. *Academic Tribes and Territories: Intellectual Enquiry and the Cultures of Disciplines.* Milton Keynes, England: Open University Press, 1989.

Biglan, A. "The Characteristics of Subject Matter in Different Academic Areas." *Journal of Applied Psychology,* 1973, 57 (3), 195–203.

Broudy, H. S. "Types of Knowledge and Purposes of Education." In R. C. Anderson, R. J. Spiro, and W. E. Montague (eds.), *Schooling and the Acquisition of Knowledge.* Hillsdale, N.J.: Erlbaum, 1977.

Donald, J. G. "Intellectual Skills in Higher Education." *Canadian Journal of Higher Education,* 1985, 15 (1), 53–68.

Donald, J. G. "Knowledge and the University Curriculum." *Higher Education,* 1986, 15 (3), 267–282.

Donald, J. G. "Learning Schemata: Methods of Representing Cognitive, Content, and Curriculum Structures in Higher Education." *Instructional Science,* 1987, 16, 187–211.

Donald, J. G. "University Professors' Views of Knowledge and Validation Processes." *Journal of Educational Psychology,* 1990, 82 (2), 242–249.

Donald, J. G. "Science Students' Learning: Ethnographic Studies in Three Disciplines." In P. Pintrich, D. Brown, and C. Weinstein (eds.), *Student Motivation, Cognition, and Learning.* Hillsdale, N.J.: Erlbaum, 1994.

Dressel, P., and Mayhew, L. *Higher Education as a Field of Study.* San Francisco: Jossey-Bass, 1974.

Frederiksen, N. "Implications of Cognitive Theory for Instruction in Problem Solving." *Review of Educational Research,* 1984, *54* (3), 363–407.

Hirsch, E. D., Jr. *Validity in Interpretation.* New Haven: Yale University Press, 1967.

Hirst, P. *Knowledge and the Curriculum: A Collection of Philosophical Papers.* London: Routledge & Kegan Paul, 1974.

King, A., and Brownell, J. *The Curriculum and the Disciplines of Knowledge.* New York: Wiley, 1966.

Krathwohl, D. R. *Social and Behavioral Science Research.* San Francisco: Jossey-Bass, 1985.

Meyers, C. *Teaching Students to Think Critically: A Guide for Faculty in All Disciplines.* San Francisco: Jossey-Bass, 1986.

Pantin, C. *The Relations Between the Sciences.* Cambridge, England: Cambridge University Press, 1968.

Popper, K. R. *The Logic of Scientific Discovery.* London: Hutchinson, 1959.

Reif, F., Larkin, J. H., and Brackett, G. C. "Teaching General Learning and Problem-Solving Skills." *American Journal of Physics,* 1976, *44* (3), 212–217.

Ricoeur, P. *Interpretation Theory: Discourse and the Surplus of Meaning.* Fort Worth: Texas Christian University Press, 1976.

Rosenberg, C. "Towards an Ecology of Knowledge: On Discipline, Context, and History." In A. Oleson and J. Voss (eds.), *The Organization of Knowledge in Modern America, 1860–1920.* Baltimore: Johns Hopkins University Press, 1979.

Skinner, Q. *The Return of Grand Theory in the Human Sciences.* Cambridge, England: Cambridge University Press, 1985.

Sternberg, R. J. "Teaching Critical Thinking, Part 1: Are We Making Critical Mistakes?" *Phi Delta Kappan,* Nov. 1985, 194–198.

Thompson, J. D., Hawkes, R. W., and Avery, R. W. "Truth Strategies and University Organization." *Educational Administration Quarterly,* 1969, *5,* 4–25.

Toulmin, S. *Human Understanding.* Vol. 1. Oxford: Clarendon Press, 1972.

*Janet G. Donald is full professor in the Department of Educational and Counselling Psychology and the Centre for University Teaching and Learning at McGill University, Montreal.*

*Two lessons from comparable undergraduate courses in physics and engineering are analyzed to identify content, issues emphasized, and concepts used. Differences reflecting the pure nature of one field (physics) versus the applied nature of the other (engineering) are identified in the two lessons.*

# What Is Taught in an Undergraduate Lecture? Differences Between a Matched Pair of Pure and Applied Disciplines

*Nira Hativa*

The best known classification of university academic fields is that of Biglan (1973), described in the Editors' Notes. A variety of studies have validated this classification, and still other studies have used it to identify disciplinary differences related to teaching and learning. Within this framework, one aspect that has been barely investigated is differences among disciplines in the type of knowledge that university instruction is supposed to produce. Do different academic areas emphasize different types of knowledge? Because the main objective in teaching is to promote student knowledge, the question of what sort of student knowledge is being produced is of major importance. Donald has done the bulk of studies on this topic (1983, 1986, 1991a, 1991b, 1993), using qualitative methods (interviews of professors and students and analysis of course materials). The study reported herein examined some of the same aspects investigated by Donald, but from a different angle, that of actual classroom instruction. By using observations of actual instruction, this study verifies and elaborates earlier findings and also reveals aspects of instruction that are not manifest from interviews or course materials.

This research is limited to just two lessons taken from a single dimension of the Biglan classification, the pure versus the applied. Pure fields are those that develop their own model or paradigm, whereas applied fields are those that use and practically extend the model or paradigms worked out by the corresponding pure field (Donald, 1991a). The two disciplines chosen were physics (pure) and engineering (applied). These two disciplines have been recognized as fields for a long period of time and thus have developed their own cultures (Donald 1991a). They also share two of Biglan's other categories, since both involve non-living systems and both are "hard" or paradigmatic. They are regarded as "matching" disciplines (Donald, 1991a) in that physics has well-developed models and paradigms and engineering applies these paradigms. The fact that these are matching pure and applied fields is reflected in university instruction, since many engineering courses apply physics principles.

To identify differences in the types of knowledge transmitted through physics and engineering instruction, we first need to categorize the types of knowledge we think exist. Donald (1986) suggests four levels of knowledge acquisition in university teaching: the nature of concepts in the field, the logical structure of the discipline, the truth criteria used, and the methods employed. Because this study was based on only a single lesson in each field, I expected that the lessons would not reflect all four levels. The first level seemed the most appropriate for analysis because terms and concepts are used explicitly throughout each physics and engineering lesson.

Concepts play a major role in learning in a discipline. A concept is organized information that is not dependent on immediate perception and is at least potentially nameable (Nelson, 1977). The purpose of a concept is to clarify and stabilize thinking through categorization or organization of some kind (Donald, 1986). Donald (1983, 1986) investigated several aspects of disciplinary differences in key concepts among several academic areas. The main aspects were the relative number and types of key concepts involved, the familiarity and definition of these concepts, and their level of generality and abstractness.

## Choosing and Analyzing the Lectures

Two undergraduate lecture courses, required for students majoring in the respective departments, were chosen in order to reflect the core type of knowledge taught in courses of each discipline and to optimally match one another.

The study took place in the departments of physics and electrical engineering at Stanford University during the 1994–95 academic year. By pure luck, two courses that satisfied the considerations outlined above were each being taught by an award-winning teacher. Both teachers were males, removing gender as a variable. Analysis of their syllabi revealed that these two courses matched in several other respects: (1) both shared the same core topic, quantum mechanics; (2) both courses were required in the third year for majors (that is, for juniors) but were also taken by sophomores; and (3) both courses required as prerequisites or conquisites several other courses in their respective disciplines as well as the same mathematics course. Thus we may view these two courses as matching to a high degree, although they were in two different departments.

Examination of the two departments' published curricula and syllabi reveals, however, that there is a substantial difference between the departments in the way that courses for the major are structured and in the number of courses that are prerequisite or conquisite for the two courses in our study. Physics majors are required to take in the first two years, as a prerequisite to the course chosen for this study, a sequence of thirteen courses: nine from physics and four from mathematics. In engineering, students take many courses in physics, chemistry, and mathematics during the first two years, but only a few basic courses in engineering. The core specialization in a particular field of engineering, for example in electrical engineering, starts with the third year. Thus, the engineering course in this study required a sequence of only five prerequisite or conquisite courses: an introductory engineering course (prerequisite), a concurrent course in electrical engineering, a physics course, and two mathematics courses. The latter three courses were also included in the prerequisite sequence of courses for the physics course studied.

The full engineering course was videotaped, as a part of a program that broadcasts courses to employees in local high-technology companies. Of the twenty-seven videotaped lessons in that course, through a random procedure the sixth lesson was chosen for analysis. In line with that choice, the sixth lecture in the physics course was specially videotaped for this study. In addition, these two lessons were transcribed. Using both the videotapes and the transcriptions, the lessons were qualitatively analyzed by the author, who has some knowledge of mathematics and physics at the university level, and by a doctoral physics student, who had taken several undergraduate electrical engineering courses. The results reported below reflect only those conclusions agreed upon by both of these judges. A computer software program was used to count the frequency of occurrence of particular terms in each lesson and the total number of words and paragraphs. The first five lessons, those preceding lesson number six, were also transcribed and studied for the engineering course; for the physics course, the first five lessons were analyzed through the instructor's very detailed class notes. The physics instructor was also interviewed regarding these lessons.

## Analysis of the Lessons' Content

Each segment of each lesson was analyzed to identify its main purpose, and then the content of the whole lesson was summarized in general terms, as follows.

*The physics lesson* concentrated on a set of computational techniques within the quantum mechanics framework that can be implemented on the computer. The instructor defined these techniques as very powerful because they produce numbers that compare favorably with the predictions of experimental results. The ability to predict numerically the results of experiments is the ultimate goal of physics, as emphasized by this instructor. The first part of the lesson introduced the central computational method in general terms, presenting its objectives, advantages, usefulness, and practical applications. This was followed by a proof consisting of a long mathematical derivation.

The second part concentrated on the application of the new technique to proving certain mathematical properties. The third part provided several

numerical examples and applications of the new technique to solving problems that students had already studied in previous courses. Each of these solutions consisted of mathematical derivations, followed by several special cases
of the properties identified. The lesson concluded with a summary and a general overview of the techniques.

Throughout the mathematical derivations of the third part of the lesson,
several additional techniques were introduced to simplify the computations or
to optimize them. The mathematical derivations were each presented along
with a rough graph of the functions involved; the instructor's explanations then
linked the elements of the mathematical derivations to these graphs. In several
cases, the instructor used analogies linking the functions to students' daily life
experiences in order to promote their intuition and understanding.

*The engineering lesson* objectives, as defined by the instructor, were to help
students understand how semiconductor devices and circuits work. The instructor used two models to qualitatively explain the internal structure and its
processes: a three-dimensional physical model and a pictorial model. Every so
often the instructor noted that the concepts and processes he was presenting
were used in electronic devices and, moreover, "are crucial for making devices."

The major part of the lesson concentrated on a qualitative description and
explanation of the central process, using the two models alternatively. The
process described the movement of electrons in the semiconductor lattice at
differing energy levels and temperatures. Several new terms and concepts were
presented and defined during the development of the explanation, all based
on various aspects of the process. Several special cases of the process were discussed, each building on the previous ones. The instructor sharpened the concepts by presenting a few cases in which the process did not work.

The last part of the lesson presented a quantitative aspect of the process.
The instructor started this part by presenting two equations and explaining
only roughly the physics on which their derivation was based; he did not
derive them mathematically. The instructor emphasized several times that these
equations were in fact the key/important results of the quantitative development, that they were used a lot in calculating the properties of devices, and
that the focus in the course was on understanding how to use these equations,
not how to derive them mathematically. Then the instructor explained what
each term in the equations stood for, presented graphically several possible
outcomes of the computations using these equations, and interpreted the
graphs in the different cases. He also added some physical interpretation and
concluded by summarizing the topics presented.

## Analysis of the Lessons' Components

Although the length of the two lessons was almost the same (fifty-one minutes
for physics and fifty for engineering), the engineering professor said more:
7,638 words in seventy-eight paragraphs for engineering as compared with
7,232 words in sixty-five paragraphs for physics. This is probably the result of

the engineering professor's effective use of an overhead projector and transparencies (copies of which the students received before the day of the class), which enabled him to speak rather than write on the board. The physics professor used time to write full derivations on the board; however, he too gave his students class notes in advance, at the beginning of the session. The notes for both classes were very detailed and included textual explanations in addition to the mathematical derivations. However, the engineering professor presented a lot of redundant information, whereas the physics instructor very seldom repeated. Thus, I estimate that a comparable amount of information was presented in both lessons.

**Analysis of Terms and Concepts Presented.** The concepts presented were analyzed using qualitative methods. Results are summarized in Table 2.1.

Table 2.1 reveals that, coincidentally, both lessons used exactly the same number (123) of different specialized terms and concepts. However, the engineering professor used them much more often (748 times) than the physics professor did (547 times), probably because of the former's larger amount of oral communication and repetition. On the other hand, within the total number of different terms and concepts, the physics lesson included more generic terms and concepts (95) than the engineering lesson (73). I consider as "generic" those terms and concepts that do not consist of a combination of other terms that have already been mentioned in the lesson. To illustrate, in the engineering lesson, the term *band*, used to explain a particular feature in a model, was counted as generic whereas the terms *band diagrams, band gap,* and *band model* that followed were counted as nongeneric. Having more generic terms suggests overall a larger number of different concepts.

The engineering course used significantly more new terms and concepts from the first six lessons of the course than did the physics course (65 versus 9). On the other hand, the physics lesson relied much more heavily on concepts introduced in the prerequisite physics and mathematics courses (87 versus 13). This difference may be explained if we realize that the physics course came after a long sequence of mathematics and physics courses that built on previous ones in the series, while the engineering course had a different orientation from most of the previous required courses.

The physics lesson used more terms that are taught in high school advanced science and mathematics courses (42 [14 + 28] versus 30 [20 + 10]). In the physics lesson, 58 (30 + 28) of the 123 different terms and concepts, or almost one half (47 percent), related to the domain of mathematics, and 52 percent (30/58) of those were based on material taught solely at the university level. To compare, less than 10 percent of terms in the engineering lesson (12 [2 + 10] of 123) came from the domain of mathematics, and only 2 of the 12 mathematics terms were taught at the university level. Altogether, the physics lesson used five times as many terms taken from mathematics as did the engineering lesson (58 versus 12).

The number of terms that are familiar in university students' daily life was comparable (37 for physics versus 34 for engineering), but physics used a

### Table 2.1. Terms and Concepts

| | | | | | Taught in | | |
|---|---|---|---|---|---|---|---|
| | Mentioned Throughout the Lesson | | | Lesson | First 5 Lessons of | Previous University Courses | |
| Domain | Different | Total | Generic | Observed | Same Course | Physics | Math |
| Physics | 123 | 547 | 95 | 3 | 6 | 57 | 30 |
| Engineering | 123 | 748 | 73 | 21 | 44 | 11 | 2 |

| | | May Be Familiar to Students from | | | |
|---|---|---|---|---|---|
| | High School Course | | Daily Life Meaning | | Computer or Technological Experience |
| | Science | Math | Same | Different | |
| Physics | 14 | 28 | 12 | 25 | 2 |
| Engineering | 20 | 10 | 21 | 13 | 7 |

| | Miscellaneous Aspects | | | |
|---|---|---|---|---|
| | Units of Measurement | Nouns | Verbs | Named After People |
| Physics | 0 | 108 | 15 | 13 |
| Engineering | 3 | 110 | 14 | 5 |

higher proportion of different terms that are known but have a specialized meaning different from that used in daily life (25/123 [20 percent]) than engineering (13/123 [10.5 percent]). To illustrate, the following terms were used throughout these two lessons in a manner that is either somewhat or completely different from their conventional meaning: *bending, expectation, integrate, potential, acceptor,* and *holes.* All together, 114 of the 123 terms used in the physics lesson (93 percent) and 102 (83 percent) of those used in the engineering lesson were terms not used in daily life.

Still another difference was that the physics lesson used more than twice as many terms in mathematics and physics that were named after particular people, for example, the *Hamilton principle, Jacoby polynomials, Poisson's equation, Bessel functions,* as the engineering lesson did. Using titled procedures requires that students have good familiarity with the meaning and applications of each of the procedures.

In a few other aspects, there was not much difference between the two lessons. Both were similar in the number of concepts that were nouns (89 percent) or verbs (11 percent), and both had exactly the same percentage of concepts likely to be familiar to students who had had some computer or other technology experience (6 percent). There was a small difference between the two lessons in the number of units of measurement presented (0 versus 3), but these numbers are too small to draw any conclusions.

**Other Levels of Analysis.** Other aspects of domain knowledge, such as rules, laws, and models, were rarely referred to during the two lessons, and so no difference was observed in this category. The physics lesson mentioned three rules and one model, whereas the engineering lesson brought up two rules and two models.

Both instructors transmitted to their students, either explicitly or implicitly, their conceptions of the main goals for learning the course material. The physics professor emphasized the importance of understanding how the techniques presented were arrived at, how they were derived mathematically, why they were correct, and how to use them effectively for certain computations. The engineering instructor, on the other hand, emphasized the importance of understanding how electronic devices work in order to be able to make these devices. He deemphasized the need to fully understand how the formulas were derived mathematically or physically and instead emphasized the importance of when (in what cases) and how to use them.

## Summary and Discussion

This study aimed at identifying, through analysis of actual classroom instruction, differences in the types of knowledge transmitted in two matching fields, one pure (physics) and the other applied (engineering). Results show that the applied field makes substantial use of knowledge and paradigms developed in the pure field. However, there are also important differences between these lessons, reflecting their pure versus applied natures. The pure field emphasized the need to verify the correctness of every procedure with basic mathematical and physical principles and the need to thoroughly understand why procedures work. The primary aim of the computational applications in the physics lesson is the prediction of results of physical experiments. This finding agrees with those of Donald from her interviews with physics professors (1986, p. 278), that "physics courses focus on the development of inferential and verification processes" and "the process of validation in physics for theoretical physicists is by experiment" (Donald, 1991a, p. 19).

The applied domain, in contrast, emphasized the need to understand how processes work and how to apply them while accepting their correctness/validity as a given fact without any verification. Thus, engineering relies on the validity of the physical models already proved by physicists and concentrates on procedures to apply them. This core difference between the two domains dictates the other substantial differences identified in the two lessons, the most important of which are that (1) the main activities throughout the physics lesson were mathematical derivations, numerical techniques, and mathematical proofs, whereas in the engineering lesson the main activity was a very detailed description of a process; (2) the two domains interpret differently the concept of application of a theory, with this referring in the physics lesson to mathematical derivations in solving problems, whereas in the engineering lesson it meant understanding how electronic devices work; (3) the physics lesson relied heavily on knowledge of high-level mathematics and extensively used a very large number of mathematical methods, whereas the engineering lesson used only very basic mathematics and concentrated on qualitative explanations; and

(4) the physics curriculum, at least at the undergraduate third-year level, is much more sequential than the engineering curriculum and requires very wide prerequisite knowledge in science and mathematics, more substantial knowledge than the electrical engineering curriculum requires at this level.

This study identified additional aspects that may be of interest. First, the large number of terms used in the lessons that are taught in high school science and mathematics courses indicates that physical science professors expect their students to have a specific physics vocabulary and some knowledge of mathematics acquired from their high school courses (Donald, 1993). Second, many new terms and concepts are introduced in each lesson in courses close to the beginning of a sequence (as with the electrical engineering course) compared to a smaller number introduced in courses further along in the sequence (as with the physics course). Third, the teaching methods employed by both teachers were similar. These instructors used graphs as an essential part of their explanations, connected the new material to previous material taught in their course and in others, and talked about or showed how to apply the material.

## Implications for Instruction and Research

Several practical implications for instruction may be derived from these findings. First, instructors in both physics and engineering should be aware of the very large number of specialized/technical terms that they use and should review terms, concepts, and procedures that may be unfamiliar to students. The long list of concepts based on high school science and mathematics courses that are used in physics and engineering courses suggests that high school students who plan to study science or engineering at the university level (more so for physics than for engineering) need to gain a solid background in science and mathematics in high school.

Second, all professors should learn from the award-winning teachers in this study the importance of repeatedly explaining to students the main objectives of their instruction, of what it is important for students to understand.

The third implication is a suggestion about research methods for studying university instruction. The method of analysis used here, of actual classroom instruction, complements that of interviews and analyses of course material (as used by Donald, for example). Not only does this method reinforce some of the previous findings through illustrations of how these concepts are implemented in practice, but it also contributes new and beneficial information. It shows how instructors transmit the main goals of the field; it quantifies the issues identified (for example, Donald's claim [1993] that physics courses have more technical or less familiar concepts than courses in other domains); it provides additional interpretation to other issues (for example, Donald's claim [1991b] that students entering engineering programs are expected to have a background in mathematics and physics); and it presents the basic structure, content, and teaching methods in lessons in the discipline. In short, the results of this research method in the present study suggest a (partial) answer to the questions: What is taught in a lecture? What are the differences in lectures in two particular fields matched on the pure-applied dimension?

### References

Biglan, A. "The Characteristics of Subject Matter in Different Academic Areas." *Journal of Applied Psychology,* 1973, *57* (3), 195–203.

Donald, J. "Knowledge Structures: Methods for Exploring Course Content." *Journal of Higher Education,* 1983, *54* (1), 31–41.

Donald, J. "Knowledge and the University Curriculum." *Higher Education,* 1986, *15* (3), 267–282.

Donald, J. "Ethnography in the Classroom: A Comparative Study in Higher Education." Unpublished report, McGill University, 1991a.

Donald, J. "The Learning Task in Engineering Courses: A Study of Professors' Perceptions of the Learning Process in Six Selected Courses." *European Journal of Engineering Education,* 1991b, *16* (2), 181–192.

Donald, J. "Professors' and Students' Conceptualizations of the Learning Task in Introductory Physics Courses." *Journal of Research in Science Teaching,* 1993, *30* (8), 905–918.

Nelson, K. "Cognitive Development and the Acquisition of Concepts." In R. Anderson, R. J. Spiro, and W. E. Montague (eds.), *Schooling and the Acquisition of Knowledge,* 1977, 215–239.

*Nira Hativa is professor in the School of Education and faculty developer in the Natural Science and Engineering Departments at Tel Aviv University. In 1994–95 she was a visiting professor in the Department of Physics at Stanford University under a grant from the Peter and Helen Bing Fund for Teaching at Stanford.*

# PART TWO

Disciplinary Differences
in Teaching and in Teachers'
Beliefs, Attitudes,
and Perceptions

*Arts, science, and social science teachers differ in the frequency with which they exhibit specific classroom teaching behaviors. This variation may account for disciplinary differences in student ratings of instruction.*

# Disciplinary Differences in Classroom Teaching Behaviors

*Harry G. Murray, Robert D. Renaud*

Student ratings of teachers and courses have been shown to provide reliable and valid information on instructional quality in higher education. Results vary somewhat from study to study, but the weight of evidence indicates that student ratings (1) are stable across items, raters, and time periods; (2) are affected to only a minor extent by extraneous variables such as class size and severity of grading; (3) are consistent with ratings of the same teachers made by colleagues, alumni, and trained classroom observers; and, most important of all, (4) are significantly correlated with more objective indicators of teaching effectiveness, such as student performance on common final examinations in multiple-section courses (Centra, 1993; Marsh and Dunkin, 1992).

Academic discipline appears to be one area in which student ratings of teaching do differ systematically. Feldman (1978) reviewed research in this area and concluded that, on average, student ratings are highest for arts and humanities teachers, lowest for science, mathematics, and engineering teachers, and intermediate for social science teachers. Cashin (1990) reached essentially the same conclusion in an analysis of standardized student rating data for approximately one hundred thousand classes across North America.

Although there is clear and consistent evidence that student instructional ratings are higher for some academic fields (for example, humanities) than for others (for example, sciences), the reasons for these differences remain to be determined. Franklin and Theall (1992) compared teachers in humanities, business, and science and engineering in terms of instructional goals, teaching methods, and grading practices. They found that humanities teachers tended to emphasize "thought" goals more so than "fact" goals and to use discussion and independent projects rather than lecturing alone. Given that both

NEW DIRECTIONS FOR TEACHING AND LEARNING, no. 64, Winter 1995 © Jossey-Bass Publishers of these teaching practices were independently shown to correlate with student ratings, the use of these practices provides a possible explanation for higher student ratings in arts and humanities courses. Cashin (1990) suggested several other possible explanations for differences in student ratings, including student attitudes, course difficulty, and actual differences in teaching effectiveness among disciplines.

The goal of research reported in this chapter was to determine whether teachers in different academic fields differ in the frequency with which they exhibit specific classroom teaching behaviors and, if so, whether these differences could be responsible for differences in student ratings of overall teaching effectiveness. Teachers in three academic fields—namely, arts and humanities, social sciences, and natural sciences and mathematics—were systematically observed in the classroom to assess the frequency of occurrence of specific "low inference" teaching behaviors. These behaviors include asking questions of students, writing key terms on the blackboard, and addressing individual students by name. Correlations were then derived, separately for each academic field, between behavioral frequency estimates and end-of-term student ratings of teaching.

Previous research (Murray, 1983, 1985) has demonstrated strong correlations between low-inference classroom teaching behaviors and student ratings of instructional quality. Furthermore, at least one previous study (Erdle and Murray, 1986) has reported differences among academic disciplines in the frequency of low-inference teaching behaviors. The present study sought to confirm these results in a larger and more diverse sample of teachers, and to articulate more explicitly the hypothesis that classroom teaching behaviors are responsible for disciplinary differences in perceived teaching effectiveness. (For a different interpretation, see the Cashin and Downey chapter in this volume.)

## Observing 401 Teachers

The sample investigated in this study consisted of 401 faculty members teaching undergraduate lecture or lecture-discussion courses with enrollment of thirty or higher at the University of Western Ontario. Each of these individuals had participated previously in one of a series of classroom observation studies carried out by the first author, the results of which were aggregated into one archival data file for purposes of the present study. The 401 teachers could be divided into three general academic fields: arts and humanities ($n = 117$); social sciences ($n = 149$); and natural sciences and mathematics ($n = 135$).

The academic departments included in each disciplinary group are listed in Table 3.1. In terms of Biglan's (1973) taxonomy (see the Editors' Notes), the academic fields compared in this study appear to vary mostly in terms of the "hard" versus "soft" dimension.

**Classroom Observations.** Classroom teaching behaviors were assessed by trained observers who visited regular classes taught by participating instructors. Each instructor was observed by three to twelve different observers ($M = 7.45$).

**Table 3.1. Composition of Disciplinary Groups**

| Arts and Humanities | Social Sciences | Natural Sciences and Mathematics |
| --- | --- | --- |
| English | Psychology | Chemistry |
| Philosophy | Sociology | Physiology |
| French | Political science | Physics |
| Classics | Economics | Biochemistry |
| Visual arts | Geography | Geology |
| Modern languages | Anthropology | Mathematics |
| History | | Biology |
| Music | | Applied mathematics |
| | | Computer science |
| | | Anatomy |

Each observer attended three individually selected one-hour class segments taught by an instructor over a three-month period. Classroom observers were paid for their work, and before visiting classes they were given approximately four hours of training in recording low-inference teaching behaviors from videotaped samples. Instructors gave written permission for classroom observation to occur but did not know exactly when the observations would take place.

Observers summarized their three hours of observation of a given instructor on a standardized behavioral rating form called the Teacher Behaviors Inventory (TBI) (Murray, 1983). Each of the one hundred items of the TBI describes a specific low-inference teaching behavior (for example, "signals the transition from one topic to the next"; "maintains eye contact with students"), which the observer rates on a 5-point frequency-of-occurrence scale: 1 = almost never; 2 = rarely; 3 = sometimes; 4 = often; 5 = almost always. Ratings were averaged across observers to obtain mean frequency ratings of each of one hundred teaching behaviors for each of 401 instructors. The reliability of observer mean ratings of individual TBI items has averaged .75 in previous studies, indicating that classroom observers show substantial interrater agreement in their assessment of specific teaching behaviors.

**Student Ratings.** Overall teaching effectiveness of participating instructors was measured by formal end-of-term student ratings for the course in which classroom observation took place. Student evaluation of teaching is required in all courses at the University of Western Ontario, and most of the instructors included in the present study were evaluated by means of the same 10-item evaluation form with a 5-point agree-disagree rating scale. To obtain a single, comparable measure of overall teaching effectiveness for each instructor, ratings were averaged across all items of the evaluation form.

## Comparing the Disciplines

A preliminary analysis was undertaken to determine whether there were differences among arts, social science, and natural science disciplines in mean student ratings of overall teaching effectiveness. Consistent with previous studies (for example, Cashin, 1990; see also Cashin and Downey and Franklin and Theall in this volume), mean student ratings were significantly higher for arts and humanities teachers (3.96) than for social science teachers (3.82), which in turn were significantly higher than for natural science and mathematics teachers (3.69).

**Teaching Behaviors by Discipline.** In order to obtain a manageable set of teaching behavior variables for use in statistical analyses, the one hundred items from the Teacher Behaviors Inventory were grouped into factors or dimensions on the basis of factor loadings in previously reported factor analyses (Murray, 1983, 1985; Erdle and Murray, 1986). Any of the one hundred TBI items that failed to show a strong and consistent relation to a single factor was deleted. This resulted in the retention of a total of sixty-four TBI items loading on a total of ten factors. Table 3.2 shows the individual teaching behaviors defining each of the ten factors. Alpha reliability coefficients for the ten factors ranged from .63 to .88 and averaged .82, indicating a high level of internal consistency among the items constituting a particular factor. Instructors were assigned scores on each of the ten teaching behavior factors by averaging frequency-of-occurrence ratings across the individual teaching behaviors defining a particular factor.

Table 3.3 shows group mean frequency ratings of each of the ten teaching behavior factors for instructors in the three disciplinary groups, arts and humanities, social sciences, and natural sciences and mathematics. A multivariate analysis of variance showed that the disciplinary groups differed significantly with respect to the frequency of occurrence of all teaching behavior factors taken collectively. Univariate analyses of variance indicated that six of the ten factors, namely Interaction, Organization, Pacing, Disclosure, Rapport, and Mannerisms, differed significantly across academic fields. Inspection of Table 3.3 reveals that teachers of arts and humanities subjects were more likely

#### Table 3.2. Definition of Teaching Behavior Dimensions

| Clarity | Uses concrete examples |
|---|---|
| | Stresses most important points |
| | Fails to define new terms[*] |
| | Gives multiple examples |
| | Suggests memory aids |
| | Repeats difficult ideas |
| | Writes key terms on blackboard |
| | Answers student questions thoroughly |
| Expressiveness | Moves about room while teaching |
| | Gestures with hands and arms |
| | Speaks expressively or "dramatically" |
| | Exhibits facial gestures |
| | Uses humor |
| | Reads lecture verbatim from notes[*] |
| | Gestures with head or body |
| | Smiles or laughs |

| | |
|---|---|
| Interaction | Encourages students to ask questions |
| | Addresses individual students by name |
| | Asks questions of class as a whole |
| | Asks questions of individual students |
| | Praises students for good ideas |
| | Incorporates student ideas into lecture |
| | Talks with students before or after class |
| | Uses a variety of teaching methods |
| Organization | Reviews topics from previous lectures |
| | Puts outline of lecture on blackboard |
| | Gives preliminary overview of lecture |
| | Uses headings and subheadings to organize lecture |
| | Signals transition from one topic to the next |
| | Summarizes periodically |
| | Explains how each topic fits into the course |
| Pacing | Dwells excessively on obvious points* |
| | Covers very little material in class sessions* |
| | Sticks to the point in answering questions |
| | Digresses from major theme of lecture |
| | Fails to take the initiative in class* |
| Disclosure | States teaching objectives |
| | Advises students how to prepare for exams |
| | Provides sample exam questions |
| | Tells students what is expected on assignments |
| | Reminds students of test assignment dates |
| Interest | Describes personal experiences related to subject |
| | Points out practical applications of concepts |
| | Presents thought-provoking ideas |
| | Relates subject matter to student interests |
| | States own point of view on controversial issues |
| | Relates subject matter to current events |
| Rapport | Offers to help students with problems |
| | Shows interest in student ideas |
| | Announces availability for consultation |
| | Shows tolerance for other points of view |
| | Is flexible regarding deadlines and requirements |
| | Is fair and impartial in interactions with students |
| | Shows concern for student progress |
| Mannerisms | Avoids eye contact with students* |
| | Shows distracting behaviors* |
| | Rocks or sways on heels* |
| | Plays with chalk or pointer* |
| | Says "um" or "ah"* |
| Speech quality | Voice fades in midsentence* |
| | Does not speak clearly* |
| | Speaks in a monotone* |
| | Stutters, mumbles, or slurs words* |
| | Speaks too softly* |

*Negatively worded items were reverse coded in computing factor scores, such that a rating of 5 represented low-frequency occurrence of the teaching behavior in question.

than social science or natural science teachers to use behaviors in the Interaction, Rapport, and Mannerisms categories (for example, addressing individual students by name, encouraging student participation, maintaining eye contact with students), whereas teachers in the social and natural sciences were more likely than arts teachers to show behaviors loading on the Organization and Pacing factors (for example, putting outline of lecture on blackboard, sticking to the point in answering questions); and arts and natural science teachers were more likely than social science teachers to exhibit Disclosure behaviors (for example, stating teaching objectives).

In summary, the results shown in Table 3.3 support the view that teachers in different academic disciplines do in fact differ in the frequency with which they exhibit certain specific classroom teaching behaviors, with arts and humanities teachers behaving more frequently in ways that foster student participation, and natural science and social science teachers more frequently showing behaviors that facilitate structuring or organization of the subject matter.

**Teaching Behaviors and Student Ratings.** To determine whether there were differences among academic fields in the correlation of teaching behavior factors with overall teaching effectiveness, teacher mean scores on the ten teaching behavior factors were correlated separately in each disciplinary group with mean student ratings of teaching. Consistent with previous research (Murray, 1983, 1985), Table 3.4 shows strong correlations between teaching behaviors and perceived teaching effectiveness. Correlation of individual teaching behavior dimensions with overall effectiveness ranged as high as .65, and twenty-nine of the thirty correlation coefficients listed in Table 3.4 were statistically significant. However, comparison of correlation coefficients across disciplinary groups within each dimension of teaching, using Fisher's r-to-z transformation, revealed that only two of thirty pairwise differences were statistically significant. The correlation of Rapport with student instructional rating was significantly lower in

## Table 3.3. Mean Rated Frequency of Occurrence of Teaching Behaviors in Different Disciplinary Groups

| Teaching Behavior Dimension | Disciplinary Group | | |
| --- | --- | --- | --- |
| | Arts and Humanities | Social Sciences | Natural Sciences and Mathematics |
| Clarity | 3.44 | 3.57 | 3.52 |
| Expressiveness | 3.33 | 3.27 | 3.19 |
| Interaction | 3.53 | 3.08 | 2.99 |
| Organization | 2.86 | 3.21 | 3.20 |
| Pacing | 3.71 | 3.90 | 3.74 |
| Disclosure | 3.41 | 3.19 | 3.42 |
| Interest | 3.12 | 3.09 | 2.95 |
| Rapport | 4.00 | 3.76 | 3.68 |
| Mannerisms | 4.15 | 4.03 | 3.94 |
| Speech quality | 4.10 | 4.01 | 3.99 |

arts and humanities (.316) than in either social sciences (.591) or natural sciences (.579). Given that approximately 1.5 significant results would be expected by chance alone among 30 correlations, the data in Table 3.4 are best interpreted as reflecting purely random, nonsignificant group differences.

In summary, despite differences among academic fields in the frequency of occurrence of specific teaching behaviors, the contribution of these same behaviors to overall teaching effectiveness seems to be very similar in different academic fields. Although natural science teachers may be more likely to exhibit organizational behaviors than are humanities teachers, the extent to which organizational behaviors "pay off" in higher student ratings seems to be essentially the same in humanities as in natural sciences.

## Conclusions

The present research suggests that *teachers of different academic disciplines differ in the frequency with which they exhibit specific classroom teaching behaviors, but they do not differ in the correlation of these teaching behaviors with student evaluations of overall teaching effectiveness.* These findings are generally consistent with what has been reported in previous research by Solomon (1966), Pohlmann (1976), and Erdle and Murray (1986). These investigators all found behavioral differences among academic fields similar to those reported here (for example, humanities teachers encouraged student participation more than science instructors); and all found nonsignificant differences among academic fields in the correlation of specific teaching behaviors with overall teaching effectiveness.

Thus, contrary to the currently popular view (for example, Shulman, 1989) that what constitutes effective teaching is embedded in context and varies systematically from one discipline to another, research to date on specific low-inference teaching behaviors indicates that what makes an effective

Table 3.4. Correlation of Teaching Behaviors with Overall Teacher Effectiveness Rating in Different Disciplinary Groups

| Teaching Behavior Dimension | Disciplinary Group | | |
| | Arts and Humanities | Social Sciences | Natural Sciences and Mathematics |
|---|---|---|---|
| Clarity | .498 | .562 | .647 |
| Expressiveness | .308 | .402 | .446 |
| Interaction | .417 | .441 | .502 |
| Organization | .359 | .361 | .439 |
| Pacing | .511 | .464 | .609 |
| Disclosure | .254 | .405 | .220 |
| Interest | .352 | .557 | .435 |
| Rapport | .316 | .591 | .579 |
| Mannerisms | .513 | .455 | .255 |
| Speech quality | .496 | .625 | .650 |

teacher, at least in the eyes of students, is pretty much the same regardless of academic discipline. With specific reference to Shulman (1989), the present findings might be interpreted to mean that *although a teacher must have "pedagogical content knowledge" within a certain academic discipline in order to develop effective teaching activities in that discipline, it is nonetheless true that effective teachers in all disciplines tend to use the same generic teaching activities or teaching behaviors.* As a case in point, effective teachers in all academic disciplines may use concrete examples to explain concepts, but the content of these examples will vary with the discipline and will be effective only to the extent that the teacher knows how to translate the discipline into terms that students can understand. Whether these generic teaching behaviors generalize across other relevant dimensions (for example, class size, teacher and student gender) remains to be determined by further research.

Do the findings of this research provide an answer to the original question of why student ratings of teaching differ across academic disciplines? The fact that natural science and social science teachers were less likely than arts teachers to exhibit Interaction and Rapport teaching behaviors that are known to be positively correlated with student instructional ratings would seem to provide an obvious explanation of why natural science and social science teachers tend to receive lower student ratings, on average, than arts and humanities teachers. On the other hand, natural science and social science teachers were more likely than arts teachers to show teaching behaviors in the Organization and Pacing categories that are similarly known to be positively correlated with student ratings.

Perhaps the best summary statement of the present findings is that arts and humanities teachers scored higher than social science and natural science teachers on six of the ten teaching behavior dimensions listed in Table 3.3. In other words, *it appears that arts and humanities teachers tend to exhibit a wider range of teaching behaviors that contribute positively to student instructional ratings than social science or natural science teachers do,* and this finding provides one possible explanation as to why student ratings differ across academic disciplines.

## Implications for Faculty Evaluation and Faculty Development

The fact that correlations between classroom teaching behaviors and student instructional ratings were generally similar across academic disciplines has implications both for faculty evaluation and for faculty development.

The implication for faculty evaluation is that, at least with respect to courses taught by the lecture method, the factors contributing to student ratings of teaching are similar in different academic fields, and thus it is reasonable for student rating forms to be similar or perhaps even identical in content in different fields or departments.

The implication for faculty development is that it is not really necessary to focus on different teaching behaviors in working with instructors from different disciplines, but only to encourage instructors in each discipline to increase the frequency of teaching behaviors that are positively correlated with student ratings but tend, for whatever reason, to occur relatively infrequently in that discipline.

## References

Biglan, A. "The Characteristics of Subject Matter in Different Academic Areas." *Journal of Applied Psychology,* 1973, 57 (3), 195–203.

Cashin, W. E. "Students Do Rate Different Academic Fields Differently." In M. Theall and J. Franklin (eds.), *Student Ratings of Instruction: Issues for Improving Practice.* San Francisco: Jossey-Bass, 1990.

Centra, J. A. *Reflective Faculty Evaluation.* San Francisco: Jossey-Bass, 1993.

Erdle, S., and Murray, H. G. "Interfaculty Differences in Classroom Teaching Behaviors and Their Relationship to Student Instructional Ratings." *Research in Higher Education,* 1986, 24, 115–127.

Feldman, K. A. "Course Characteristics and College Students' Ratings of their Teachers: What We Know and What We Don't." *Research in Higher Education,* 1978, 9, 199–242.

Franklin, J., and Theall, M. "Disciplinary Differences: Instructional Goals and Activities, Measures of Student Performance, and Student Ratings of Instruction." Paper presented at the annual meeting of the American Educational Research Association, San Francisco, April 1992.

Marsh, H. W., and Dunkin, M. J. "Students' Evaluation of University Teaching: A Multidimensional Perspective." In J. C. Smart (ed.), *Higher Education: Handbook of Theory and Research.* Vol. 8. New York: Agathon Press, 1992.

Murray, H. G. "Low-Inference Classroom Teaching Behaviors and Student Ratings of College Teaching Effectiveness." *Journal of Educational Psychology,* 1983, 75, 138–149.

Murray, H. G. "Classroom Teaching Behaviors Related to College Teaching Effectiveness." In J. G. Donald and A. M. Sullivan (eds.), *Using Research to Improve Teaching.* San Francisco: Jossey-Bass, 1985.

Pohlmann, J. T. "A Description of Effective College Teaching in Five Disciplines as Measured by Student Ratings." *Research in Higher Education,* 1976, 4, 335–346.

Shulman, L. S. "Toward a Pedagogy of Substance." *American Association for Higher Education Bulletin,* 1989, 41 (10), 8–13.

Solomon, D. "Teacher Behavior Dimensions, Course Characteristics, and Student Evaluations of Teachers." *American Educational Research Journal,* 1966, 3, 35–47.

*Harry G. Murray is professor of psychology in the Department of Psychology, University of Western Ontario, London, Canada.*

*Robert D. Renaud is a graduate student in the Department of Psychology, University of Western Ontario, London, Canada.*

*Disciplinary differences and the value students place on the time they spend preparing for class are correlated with students' evaluations of teaching and may offer clues to how faculty can improve instructional outcomes and thus their own ratings.*

# The Relationship of Disciplinary Differences and the Value of Class Preparation Time to Student Ratings of Teaching

*Jennifer Franklin, Michael Theall*

Faculty and administrators who use ratings as a source of information when evaluating teaching worry that certain course, student, and teacher variables influence or bias ratings. For the past decade, we have been concerned about how ratings are used by faculty, administrators, and academic professionals, and how their practice can be improved or assisted with usable knowledge based on research findings.

Our studies (Franklin and Theall, 1992, 1993) have found disciplinary differences to be important factors affecting ratings in ways previously unreported. Also, a recent development in ratings research reported by Gillmore (1994) has provided a new and tantalizing clue to how ratings "work" and may lead to some valuable insights for users of ratings: the more students value the time they spend preparing for class, the higher the overall instructor ratings they give the teacher of that class. In this chapter, we combine these factors in a further effort to discuss how ratings work.

Instead of asking students to rate course workload directly, Gillmore (1994) asked how many hours students spent preparing for class and how many of those hours were perceived by students as valuable. We refer to the ratio of these variables as "time-valued." Gillmore's result was a positive correlation approaching .50 between overall ratings and time-valued. Moreover, the time-valued ratio does a much better job of explaining variation in overall ratings than the other, more traditional variables used in the study (for example, class size, course level, required versus elective course status, student and instructor gender, and instructor rank). These are characterized by correlations ranging from less than .05 to not much more than .20 in most studies.

As a result of Gillmore's findings, we included the same two items—hours spent preparing and number of those hours considered valuable—in the campuswide ratings instruments at two large research universities to learn whether the same relationship would hold true and whether time-valued would do a better job of explaining variation in overall ratings than the traditionally cited sources of systematic variation described above, which, to simplify discussion, we refer to as course/student/teacher variables. The preliminary results of our inquiry are striking and suggest many possibilities for improving practice. We have taken particular care to consider the implications in terms of disciplinary differences.

We simplified our task by breaking down the relatively abstract and speculative problems of understanding the systematic variation in ratings into three questions: (1) which variables are related to overall ratings? (2) how much variation in overall ratings do these variables and Gillmore's time-valued explain? and (3) do disciplines differ in the amount of variation in overall ratings explained by the variables and by Gillmore's time-valued ratio?

We used student ratings data collected in over eight thousand course-sections in a large, multidisciplinary research university to demonstrate some practical and theoretical implications of the most commonly cited course/student/teacher variables compared with time-valued as predictors of overall ratings of a teacher's effectiveness. We did our analysis in two stages, first looking at disciplinary differences in patterns of association between the first set of variables and overall ratings of instructor effectiveness and then, for comparative purposes, repeating each analysis but including the time-valued ratio.

To show how patterns and magnitudes of association among these variables varied by course discipline, we split the data into disciplinary groups and repeated each analysis in order to make direct comparisons across the proportions of variance in overall instructor effectiveness accounted for by each of our predictor variables in each discipline.

## Disciplinary Differences in Instructor Ratings

In the first stage of our analysis, we examined disciplinary differences in overall ratings to determine whether nonchance differences among disciplines existed. Table 4.1 shows disciplinary differences in our data.

In Table 4.1, the rank order of ratings in the Mean column is consistent with past results (Cashin, 1990). Professors in fine arts, humanities, and health-related professions are more highly rated than their science, engineering, and math-related colleagues. One striking pattern that appears in Table 4.1 is the number of significant differences occurring between pairs of disciplines. Of the fifty-five possible pairs, significant differences between disciplines occurred for all but sixteen, demonstrating considerable variation in interdisciplinary ratings in general. Some pairs of disciplines were not expected

Table 4.1. Disciplinary Differences in Overall
Instructor Effectiveness Ratings[**]

| | Mean | HE | HU | FA | AG | ED | SB | AR | SC | BU | EN | MA |
|---|---|---|---|---|---|---|---|---|---|---|---|---|
| Health-related professions (HE) | 4.36 | | * | * | * | * | * | * | * | * | * | * |
| Humanities (HU) | 4.14 | | | — | — | — | * | * | * | * | * | * |
| Fine arts (FA) | 4.11 | | | | — | — | * | * | * | * | * | * |
| Agriculture (AG) | 4.06 | | | | | — | * | — | * | * | * | * |
| Education (ED) | 4.02 | | | | | | * | — | * | * | * | * |
| Social/behavioral sciences (SB) | 3.89 | | | | | | | — | — | * | * | * |
| Architecture (AR) | 3.86 | | | | | | | | — | — | — | * |
| Sciences (SC) | 3.81 | | | | | | | | | — | * | * |
| Business/public administration (BU) | 3.74 | | | | | | | | | | — | * |
| Engineering (EN) | 3.68 | | | | | | | | | | | — |
| Mathematics/ statistics (MA) | 3.63 | | | | | | | | | | | |

[*]A significant difference was observed between this pair of disciplines ($p < .01$ or less).
—No significant difference was observed between this pair of disciplines.
[**]Mean score based on 1.0 ("among the least effective") to 5.0 ("among the most effective"); starred items significant at .05 or better.

to be significantly different because they lie at the same extremes of the ratings scale (for example, fine arts and humanities, or mathematics and engineering).

## How Important Are the Course/Student/Teacher and Time-Valued Variables?

We also explored the relative importance of course/student/teacher and time-valued variables for explaining variation in overall instructor ratings. Our findings appear in Table 4.2.

Three themes emerge in Table 4.2. First, the relationships among class size, course level, instructor rank, and student and teacher gender (respectively and in terms of overall ratings) are strikingly different from discipline to discipline, suggesting that these variables are not related to ratings in the same way in each discipline. Second, the time-valued ratio varies by discipline in its strength as a predictor variable. Third, except in the health-related professions, the time-valued ratio is a more powerful predictor than the other variables in every discipline.

Table 4.3 shows how much variation in ratings is explained by the combined variables in each discipline. Three themes similar to those observed in Table 4.2 emerge. First, the total amount of variance accounted for ($R^2$, multiple [R] squared) in overall ratings by the combined predictor variables of class size, course level, instructor rank, and student and teacher gender ranges from about 1 percent (humanities) to 14 percent (health-related professions). The

Table 4.2.  Disciplinary Differences in the Impact of Variables on Prediction of Overall Ratings of Instructor Teaching Effectiveness*

| | Class Size | Course Level | Percent of Students Taking Course as Requirement | Instructor Rank | Percent Female Students | Instructor Gender | Time-Value Ratio |
|---|---|---|---|---|---|---|---|
| Health-related professions | | | −.32 | | | | .24 |
| Humanities | −.20 | | | | | | .35 |
| Fine arts | | | | | −.20 | | .42 |
| Agriculture | −.17 | | | | | | .42 |
| Education | | | | −.24 | | | .67 |
| Social/behavioral sciences | −.09 | | | .07 | .07 | | .52 |
| Architecture | | | | | | n/a | |
| Sciences | | | | | | | .61 |
| Business/public administration | | | | | | | .47 |
| Engineering | | | | | | .11 | .65 |
| Mathematics/ statistics | −.14 | | | | .13 | | .64 |

*Regression beta weights (rounded) showing relative strength of predictor variables; all "time-valued" betas significant (T) at $p < .0001$ with the exception of health-related professions ($p < .03$); all other betas significant (T) at $p < .03$ or $p < .01$.

second theme is that the amount of variation in overall ratings explained by time-valued combined with the first set of variables varies widely by discipline, ranging from 12 percent (humanities) to 45 percent (mathematics and statistics). The third and most striking pattern to emerge in Table 4.3 is the total proportion of variance in overall ratings accounted for when the time-valued ratio is added to the other predictor variables (except for agriculture and health-related professions).

## Implications for Users of Student Ratings

Here, we explore implications for those who use student ratings to make personnel decisions, to improve their teaching, or as the subject of their research.

**For Personnel Decision Making.** These results should hold particular interest for faculty and administrators who use ratings to document teaching quality as regards promotion, tenure, or merit decisions. The first conclusion that seems obvious to us is that the variation across disciplines found here strongly reconfirms the conventional wisdom that it is inadvisable to compare instructors or courses across disciplines.

The next conclusion suggested by these data also confirms the general feeling that under most circumstances, the small but significant associations found between most commonly reported sources of systematic variation

**Table 4.3. Total Percent Variance in Overall Instructor Ratings Explained by Predictor Variables Across Disciplines***

| Course Discipline | $R^2$ for All Variables Except "Time-Valued" | $R^2$ for All Variables Including "Time-Valued" |
|---|---|---|
| Health-related professions | .14 | .16 |
| Humanities | .01 | .12 |
| Fine arts | .08 | .21 |
| Agriculture | .04 | .21 |
| Education | NAP | .42 |
| Social/behavioral sciences | .04 | .29 |
| Architecture | NAP | NAP |
| Sciences | NAP | .37 |
| Business/public administration | .02 | .21 |
| Engineering | .03 | .43 |
| Mathematics/statistics | .05 | .45 |

*Two-phase stepwise multiple regressions used; columns show percent of variance accounted for (multiple correlation squared, $R^2$); column one values (without "time-valued") are significant at $p < .05$ or $p < .01$; column two values (with "time-value") are significant at $p < .0001$; "NAP" indicates that no analysis was possible because of small sample size or lack of full set of predictor variables.

account for such a small proportion of variance in overall ratings that they should not be a cause for concern under most circumstances. However, having said that, we are instantly reminded of an analysis (Franklin and Theall, 1993) we performed using the data collected in another large, multidisciplinary research university. We found that significant differences (.3 in mean scores on overall ratings for male and female faculty) in a particular discipline persisted even after all other variables such as class size and required-versus-elective status were controlled. We felt that these differences were due to possible bias in teaching assignments and a departmental dynamic which put female faculty at a disadvantage, rather than being evidence of less-effective teaching by women. Although .3 is not a huge difference, in the hands of ill-informed decision makers using raw mean scores (Franklin and Theall, 1989) a pattern of systematic sex discrimination in decision making based on ratings could exacerbate the apparent discriminatory pattern of assigning large, introductory courses to women and small, upper-level seminars to men.

Similarly, as shown in Table 4.2, any of the first set of variables that has a significant beta weight should also alert ratings users to consider the possibility that failure to control for that variable could make ratings users in particular disciplines liable to errors in the decision-making process. For example, controlling for the required-versus-elective status in education courses seems to be more advisable than in any other discipline, while the general pattern of significant differences associated with faculty rank found in other literature (Marsh, 1987) is probably similar for each discipline.

A conservative strategy to minimize the effect of variation related to class size, course level, required-versus-elective status, and student and teacher gender shown in Table 4.2 would be for each discipline to compare courses within separate groups based on those specific parameters whenever practical. Alternatively, for example, one could show the relative rank of a teacher within a comparison group controlling statistically for the variables that have significant beta weights in that discipline. Happily, these alternatives are consistent with the best advice offered in the ratings literature.

**For Teaching Improvement.** Another conclusion that we can draw from these findings should be of particular interest to faculty and teaching improvement consultants. Every teacher who receives a low time-valued ratio and low ratings should ask two questions: (1) Is the work I assign actually valuable, that is, capable of contributing to students' achieving important course goals? and (2) If the work I assign is valuable, why do the students fail to perceive its value? These questions are important, because they are based on the fact that time-valued is a strong predictor of overall ratings of teaching effectiveness, which are in turn correlated with student achievement (that is, real learning as demonstrated in Cohen's meta-analysis [1981] showing an average .45 correlation between overall ratings and student performance on final exams).

We recommend that the time-valued item be included in ratings questionnaires used for both personnel decision making and teaching improvement, but particularly the latter. Teaching improvement consultants would likely find a valuable source of insight in time-valued ratios, and although we admit that we have not established a causal relationship between time-valued and ratings, it seems very likely that faculty who can improve the quality of the time students spend preparing for class would reap some benefit in higher ratings.

Certainly, one additional conclusion that might be drawn from these data is the need for faculty and teaching improvement consultants to expand their definition of effective teaching beyond the in-class presentation and delivery skills probed by typical rating questionnaires, and also to address the question of effective course design.

**For Researchers.** These findings also suggest intriguing possibilities for research. For example, why do some students fail to perceive the potential value of some instructional activities? Time spent preparing for class requires more learner involvement than does passively attending class. Our research on student ratings and student attributions of success and failure ratings (Theall, Franklin, and Ludlow, 1990) suggests that students generally exhibit internal locus of control, that is, they attribute their success or failure to their own efforts or ability. However, under extreme circumstances, in the classes rated "best" and "worst" by students on average, attributions can become more external, that is, crediting or blaming the teacher or fellow students. Not doing assigned preparations because "they are a waste of time" attributes the student's internal lack of effort to an external cause (the work itself or the professor). Perceptions of the value of time spent should also logically be related to students' pragmatism, achievement motivation, need for affiliation, and other variables. There are certainly many more relevant questions about students. For example, do students in applied professional disciplines more readily perceive the value of time spent in activities that prepare them for careers rather than the value of time spent exploring abstract theories in out-of-major courses taken solely to satisfy university requirements? Do such perceptions influence the ratings students give their teachers and courses? We believe so.

There are also many relevant questions about the characteristics of courses and how they are taught. For example, when is the *perception* of the value of preparation independent of the actual value of preparation? Faculty and researchers will find interesting a fundamental question: of the specific things that teachers do, which influence students' perceptions of time-valued? For example, among teaching behaviors measured by typical ratings instruments, those items related to clarity, interaction/feedback, and inspiring interest in the content of the course emerge as strong predictors or elements of effective teaching. Which teaching behaviors best predict time-valued?

## Conclusion

Given the strong contrast between the amount of variation in ratings accounted for by the student/course/teacher variables described in this chapter and Gillmore's time-valued variable, it seems clear to us that concentrating on increasing the value of student time spent preparing for class could very likely benefit everyone. There is much to learn about how faculty can increase the value of the time students spend on a class. Success in increasing time-valued very likely depends on faculty's ability to improve the design, implementation, and delivery of the courses they offer (Stark and others, 1988).

The final and, frankly, most speculative suggestion of these findings (considering the power of the time-valued variable to predict overall ratings) is that researchers and ratings practitioners might do well to look for more variables that directly reflect the quality of instructional design and implementation, that is, course plans and how they actually come to life. There may be other powerful predictors lurking out there that will increase the value and meaning of student feedback for every kind of ratings user and that will also decrease the likelihood of inadvertent misuse of ratings data whenever they are offered as evidence of effective teaching.

## References

Cashin, W. E. "Students Do Rate Different Academic Fields Differently." In M. Theall and J. Franklin (eds.), *Student Ratings of Instruction: Issues for Improving Practice.* New Directions for Teaching and Learning, no. 43. San Francisco: Jossey Bass, 1990.

Cohen, P. A. "Student Ratings of Instruction and Student Achievement: A Meta-Analysis of Multisection Validity Studies." *Review of Educational Research,* 1981, *31* (3), 281–309.

Franklin, J., and Theall, M. "Who Reads Ratings: Knowledge, Attitudes, and Practices of Users of Student Ratings of Instruction." Paper presented at the annual meeting of the American Educational Research Association, San Francisco, April 1989.

Franklin, J., and Theall, M. "Disciplinary Differences: Instructional Goals and Activities, Measures of Student Performance, and Student Ratings of Instruction." Paper presented at the annual meeting of the American Educational Research Association, San Francisco, April 1992.

Franklin, J., and Theall, M. "Student Ratings of Instruction and Sex Differences Revisited." Paper presented at the annual meeting of the American Educational Research Association, Atlanta, April 1993.

Gillmore, G. "The Effects of Course Demands and Grading Leniency on Student Ratings of Instruction." Paper presented at the annual meeting of the American Educational Research Association, Atlanta, April 1994.

Marsh, H. W. "Students' Evaluations of University Teaching: Research Findings, Methodological Research." *International Journal of Education Research*, 1987, *11*, 253–388.

Stark, J. S., Lowther, M. A., Ryan, M. P., Bornotti, S. S., Genthon, M., Haven, C. L., and Martens, G. *Reflections on Course Planning: Faculty and Students Consider Influences and Goals.* Technical report no. 88. Ann Arbor, Mich.: National Center for Research to Improve Postsecondary Teaching and Learning, 1988.

Theall, M., Franklin, J., and Ludlow, L.H. "Attributions and Retributions: Student Ratings and the Perceived Causes of Performance." Paper presented at the annual meeting of the American Educational Research Association, April 1990.

*Jennifer Franklin is coordinator for instructional assessment and faculty evaluation at the University of Arizona, Tucson.*

*Michael Theall is associate professor at the University of Alabama at Birmingham School of Education.*

*Disciplinary and institutional differences in the importance faculty attach to alternative goals for undergraduate education are examined, and implications are discussed for curricular and pedagogical interventions.*

# Disciplinary and Institutional Differences in Undergraduate Education Goals

John C. Smart, Corinna A. Ethington

Concern about the quality of undergraduate education has been acute for over a decade. Several critical national reports from the early 1980s focused on deficiencies of undergraduate education and proposed sweeping curricular reforms involving both content and educational processes. What is curiously missing from the reports is a recognition of the inter- and intrainstitutional diversity of colleges and universities that is the distinguishing characteristic of American higher education. The reports treat undergraduate education in the United States as if it were a monolithic entity; they ignore the distinctive purposes of different types of institutions and the different cognitive styles of academic disciplines.

The Association of American Colleges (AAC) represents an exception to this common practice of not differentiating among the distinctive disciplinary perspectives. The AAC engaged task forces composed of teaching scholars from a dozen disciplines to examine disciplinary variation in four components of undergraduate education curriculum: curricular coherence, critical perspectives, connected learning, and inclusiveness. The task force reports were published in a two-volume set (Association of American Colleges, 1991a, 1991b). A subsequent analysis of these reports by Lattuca and Stark (1994) revealed dramatic disciplinary differences in virtually every component. The lone exception to the diversity was that "the task forces from all disciplinary groupings called for autonomy in goal setting" and "tended to treat goals as departmental objectives to be articulated locally" (p. 410). In essence, the discipline-based task forces agreed to disagree and to reserve the right to define the undergraduate education curriculum from the distinctive perspectives of their respective disciplines.

Academic disciplines exist in different types of colleges and universities, and the distinctive missions of these institutions may work to enhance or diminish discipline-based tendencies. Thus, the distinctive disciplinary perspectives regarding undergraduate education curriculum noted by Lattuca and Stark (1994, 1995) must be considered within the institutional contexts within which the respective disciplines exist, for it is quite possible that those differences are not consistent across the diverse types of colleges and universities. To neglect either the disciplinary or the institutional context is to paint an incomplete, and potentially misleading, picture of undergraduate education in American higher education.

Efforts to reshape or reform undergraduate education in response to the criticisms leveled in the numerous national reports in the past decade depend upon knowledge of the disciplinary and institutional diversity noted above, for the management of diversity is at the heart of American higher education. It would seem profitable, given the premises of most planning models, to begin the quest for reform by developing understanding about how undergraduate education goals differ across the distinct disciplinary and institutional sectors. The emphasis upon goals seems reasonable because of their centrality to successful reform efforts and the fact that broad curricular goals have implications for subsequent consideration of curricular content and pedagogical methods.

Our examination of the goals of undergraduate education is guided by the Carnegie Foundation (1987) typology of postsecondary institutions and Biglan's typology (1973) of academic disciplines.

The former classifies institutions into four broad categories based primarily on the level of their degree offerings and research emphasis. The first Carnegie category, research and doctoral-granting universities, is self-explanatory. Comprehensive colleges and universities offer educational programs through the master's degree and have a minimal research emphasis. Liberal arts colleges are baccalaureate institutions with little or no research emphasis. And two-year colleges are open-admissions institutions offering developmental, community, and transfer instruction.

The Biglan typology classifies academic disciplines on the basis of their level of paradigm development (hard versus soft), concern with practical application (pure versus applied), and degree of involvement with living or organic objects of study (life versus nonlife). (See Cashin and Downey in this volume for examples of the disciplines in each Biglan cluster.)

Both typologies have been used extensively in prior research and their validity is well established.

## The Carnegie Foundation Survey

We used the 1989 Carnegie Foundation faculty survey to examine institutional and disciplinary differences in faculty members' opinions of desired outcomes of undergraduate education. Of the respondents to the survey, we selected only those faculty who regularly taught undergraduate students and classified them according to their Carnegie institutional type and the Biglan disciplinary classifications. The sample used in the analyses consisted of 4,072 faculty.

A question on the survey asked respondents to indicate the importance of each of seven proposed goals for undergraduate education. These were rated on a scale from 1 = very important to 4 = very unimportant. After reverse coding the items, a principal-components analysis with oblique rotation reduced the seven items to three factors.

*Knowledge acquisition.* The first factor was defined by three of the seven goals: provide an appreciation of literature and the arts, provide a basic understanding in mathematics and science, and provide knowledge of history and the social sciences. This factor represents the acquisition of multidisciplinary knowledge that most often comprises the general education component of undergraduate programs.

*Knowledge application.* The second factor reflected a focus on depth of knowledge and its application to career development. It was defined by two of the seven Carnegie survey goals: prepare students for a career, and provide knowledge of one subject in depth.

*Knowledge integration.* The third factor was also defined by two goals: shape students' values, and enhance creative thinking. This factor reflects the integration and use of knowledge in shaping students' thinking.

Factor scores resulting from the analysis were transformed to $T$-scores for ease of interpretation ($T$-scores are standardized measures having a mean of 50 and standard deviation of 10). We then compared the importance of these three goal factors of undergraduate education for faculty across the Carnegie institutional types and across the Biglan disciplinary classifications through a $4 \times 2 \times 2 \times 2$ multivariate analysis of variance. When a multivariate test proved to be significant, univariate ANOVAs were conducted followed by Tukey HSD tests for post hoc pairwise comparisons.

The results of our analyses (see Tables 5.1 and 5.2) revealed broad differences in the importance placed on the three undergraduate education goal factors, based upon both the disciplinary and institutional affiliations of faculty with effect sizes ranging from small (.137) to moderately large (.437). The effect sizes are given in Table 5.2 and represent the differences between pairs of means expressed in standard deviation units; thus, an effect size of .437 indicates that two group means differed by .437 standard deviations.

## Discipline Comparisons

First we review the relation between the Biglan dimensions and the goal factors. This is followed by a review of the relation between the Carnegie institutional categories and the goal factors.

**Existence of a Paradigm.** Faculty affiliated with hard and soft disciplines place differing importance on the three undergraduate education goal factors

### Table 5.1. Undergraduate Education Goal Factor Means[*]

| | Main Effect Means | | |
| | Undergraduate Education Goal Factors | | |
| | Knowledge Acquisition | Knowledge Application | Knowledge Integration |
|---|---|---|---|
| Carnegie types | | | | *n* |
| Research | 49.7 (10.3) | 49.7 (10.1) | 49.0 (10.4) | 1,660 |
| Comprehensive | 49.9 (9.7) | 50.5 (10.1) | 50.3 (9.8) | 2,016 |
| Liberal arts | 51.5 (9.5) | 49.3 (9.4) | 51.4 (9.3) | 971 |
| Two-year | 47.7 (10.3) | 51.7 (10.4) | 50.1 (10.0) | 425 |
| | | | | |
| Biglan dimensions | | | | |
| Existence of a paradigm | | | | |
| Hard | 48.9 (9.9) | 52.2 (9.6) | 48.8 (9.8) | 1,181 |
| Soft | 50.4 (10.0) | 49.1 (10.0) | 50.5 (10.1) | 2,891 |
| Concern with application | | | | |
| Pure | 52.0 (9.5) | 48.5 (9.6) | 48.8 (10.2) | 2,162 |
| Applied | 47.8 (10.1) | 51.7 (10.1) | 51.4 (9.5) | 1,910 |
| Concern with life systems | | | | |
| Life | 49.6 (10.1) | 50.7 (10.0) | 49.4 (10.0) | 1,343 |
| Nonlife | 50.2 (9.9) | 49.7 (10.0) | 50.3 (10.0) | 2,729 |

| | | Interaction Means | |
| | | Application | Integration |
|---|---|---|---|
| Life | Hard | 49.3 (10.0) | 50.2 (9.0) |
| | Soft | 49.7 (10.2) | 49.0 (10.5) |
| Nonlife | Hard | 48.7 (9.9) | 48.1 (10.1) |
| | Soft | 50.8 (9.9) | 51.1 (9.8) |

[*]Standard deviations are given in parentheses.

considered in this study. Faculty in hard disciplines place greater importance on Knowledge Application than do their colleagues in soft disciplines. Differences between faculty in hard and soft disciplines on the importance associated with Knowledge Acquisition and Knowledge Integration, however, are present only in nonlife disciplines. Of the eleven possible interactive effects, the multivariate tests were significant for only the paradigm-by-life interaction term. Subsequent univariate tests revealed that interactive effects were present only for Knowledge Acquisition and Knowledge Integration goal factors, and simple main-effect analyses indicated that within nonlife disciplines faculty in soft fields place greater importance on Knowledge Acquisition and Knowledge Integration than do faculty in hard fields. Faculty in hard and soft disciplines in life-system fields assign equal importance to these two undergraduate education goal factors.

    The greater emphasis placed on Knowledge Application by faculty in hard disciplines may be a function of the greater maturity of these fields and the fact

Table 5.2. Effect Sizes for Significant Pairwise Comparisons[*]

| | Undergraduate Education Goal Factors | | |
| --- | --- | --- | --- |
| | Knowledge Acquisition | Knowledge Application | Knowledge Integration |
| Carnegie types | | | |
| Research/comprehensive | — | — | .137 |
| Research/liberal arts | .184 | — | .251 |
| Research/two-year | .208 | .210 | — |
| Comprehensive/liberal arts | .164 | — | — |
| Comprehensive/two-year | .227 | — | — |
| Liberal arts/two-year | .392 | .251 | — |
| Biglan dimensions | | | |
| Existence of a paradigm | | | |
| Hard/soft | — | .327 | — |
| Concern with application | | | |
| Pure/applied | .437 | .338 | .265 |
| Concern with life systems | | | |
| Life/nonlife | — | — | — |
| | Interaction Mean Comparisons | | |
| Hard/soft within nonlife | .211 | — | .313 |

[*]Blank entries denote nonsignificant comparisons.

that they evidence greater consensus, more structure, and higher predictability than soft disciplines (Lattuca and Stark, 1995). Given that the knowledge base of soft fields is less mature than in hard fields and that there is less agreement among faculty in soft fields on the relative importance of problems to study and appropriate methods for investigating problems, faculty in soft disciplines may be less inclined to attach as much importance to the practical application of knowledge as their colleagues in hard disciplines do. We have no basis for speculation as to why differences between faculty in hard and soft disciplines in terms of the importance they attach to Knowledge Acquisition and Knowledge Integration exist only in nonlife fields. What our findings do suggest, however, is the importance of including all three dimensions of the Biglan typology in analyses of faculty attitudes and behaviors, since these dimensions are not independent.

**Concern with Application.** Faculty classified according to the pure versus applied nature of their disciplines differ in the importance they attach to all three undergraduate education goal factors. Faculty in pure disciplines place greater importance on Knowledge Acquisition than do faculty in applied disciplines, while the latter attach greater importance to Knowledge Application and Knowledge Integration.

The greater importance attached to Knowledge Application by faculty in applied disciplines is consistent with the nature of this dimension in Biglan's typology and with prior findings of the importance of vocational development in applied fields (Smart and Elton, 1975). However, faculty in applied fields also place greater importance on Knowledge Integration. It may be possible that the focus of attention on practical application by faculty in applied fields makes the need to synthesize and integrate existing knowledge greater than in fields where the emphasis is upon knowledge for the sake of knowledge. The greater importance that faculty in pure fields attach to sheer Knowledge Acquisition may be a function of their valuation of knowledge for the sake of knowledge.

**Involvement with Life Systems.** There are no significant differences in the importance faculty attribute to the three undergraduate education goal factors based on the life versus nonlife classifications of academic disciplines. This dimension only contributed to our understanding of disciplinary differences through its interactive effect with the paradigm dimension. The lack of differences between faculty classified according to this dimension of the Biglan typology is consistent with prior evidence that the discriminatory power of the dimension is much less than in the two other dimensions of the typology (Smart and Elton, 1975).

## Institutional Comparisons

The analyses revealed significant differences among faculty affiliated with the four general institutional categories on all three undergraduate education goal factors. These differences are consistent across all three dimensions of academic disciplines. Using Tukey for post hoc pairwise comparisons, we found different patterns of institutional differences for the three goal factors. Faculty affiliated with the Carnegie category of liberal arts colleges place more emphasis on Knowledge Acquisition than faculty in all other institutional categories, while faculty in two-year colleges place less emphasis on this goal factor than faculty in all other institutional categories. A strong emphasis on Knowledge Application is characteristic of faculty in two-year institutions, whose mean is significantly higher than that of their colleagues in either liberal arts colleges or research universities. Faculty in research universities place significantly less importance on the goal of Knowledge Integration than do those in liberal arts colleges and comprehensive colleges and universities.

Lattuca and Stark (1995) note that "those who attempt to lead curricular reform may be more successful if they recognize both the strength of disciplinary culture *and* the campus contextual factors that make faculty redefine discipline cultures to meet local needs" (p. 340, emphasis added). Their advice is fully supported by our findings of broad institutional differences that are consistent across all disciplinary classifications. The historical emphasis of liberal arts colleges on the intellectual development of students is consistent with our finding that faculty in these institutions place more importance on Knowledge Acquisition than their colleagues in the three other classifications. Similarly, the greater importance given to the Knowledge Application goal by faculty in two-year colleges seems consistent with the mission of these institutions. What is less clear is the lower importance attached to the goal of Knowledge Integration by faculty in research universities than by faculty in either liberal arts colleges or comprehensive colleges and universities. This finding may reflect the primary focus of faculty in research universities on their academic disciplines and on knowledge within the more narrow confines of those disciplines.

## Implications for Reforming Undergraduate Education

Given the goal-directed nature of most planning models, the results of our inquiry suggest that efforts to reform undergraduate education must take into consideration the rich diversity both between and within institutions that has historically characterized American higher education. Our findings clearly illustrate that faculty preferences for the emphasis placed on alternative undergraduate education goals vary as a function of both the fundamental character of the institutions in which they reside and the specific disciplines with which they are affiliated.

The focus on differences among faculty, however, may unjustly magnify diversity and leave those responsible for reform efforts with a hopeless sense of futility. What must be remembered amidst all this discussion of faculty differences and diversity is the reality that students within a specific institutional setting are exposed to diverse discipline-based course offerings. Thus, all students are faced with the challenge of developing knowledge acquisition, integration, and application skills throughout their undergraduate programs.

The challenge before those who seek to improve undergraduate education is not to engage in polemical debates about the fundamental nature or goals of undergraduate education, but rather to accept the entrenched nature of existing goals and to focus their energies and resources on assisting faculty to improve their instructional effectiveness, which ultimately will benefit student learning. Such an orientation would benefit both the general education and the specific academic major component of students' undergraduate experience, since it focuses on the distinctive emphases of academic disciplines which contribute to both components of students' total undergraduate experiences.

Within this context, the findings from our inquiry have great meaning to faculty and instructional development initiatives. They strongly suggest that reforms must consider the distinctive institutional settings and disciplinary affiliations of faculty if they are to be successful, given McKeachie's contention (1979) that teaching effectiveness represents "the degree to which one has facilitated student achievement of *educational goals*" (p. 385, emphasis added). We know also that "teaching behaviors that correlate with one outcome measure may not correlate in similar ways with other outcome measures" (Murray, 1991, p. 151). For example, Tom and Cushman (1975) suggested that teaching behaviors that promoted students' active involvement in classroom discussions tended to be related to students' development of creative thinking abilities but did not relate well to factual and conceptual knowledge growth. On the other hand, clear and well-organized lectures promoted factual knowledge but did not lead to the development of problem-solving and creative thinking abilities.

There are obvious implications, then, for the disciplinary groups that we found differing in their emphases on knowledge acquisition versus knowledge application and integration. For example, the greater emphasis placed on knowledge acquisition by faculty in pure disciplines suggests that instructional development efforts would focus more on assisting them in developing clarity and organization in their teaching. However, the manner by which one brings clarity and organization to one's teaching differs even *within* the Biglan classifications. Consider the disciplines of mathematics and English, both pure disciplines. Clarity in mathematics is often achieved through summarizing step-by-step algorithms and using tables and graphs. Factual knowledge in English is not as easily summarized in this manner. Therefore, what is effective practice leading to clarity and organization even differs for disciplines with common goal emphases—differing given the nature of the subject matter itself.

Perhaps the most important implication is based on our finding that regardless of institutional setting, academic disciplines vary in their emphases on different undergraduate education goals: those who seek to improve faculty teaching effectiveness on individual campuses should not seek global solutions or utilize uniform practices. Rather, they should work within disciplinary clusters and focus on pedagogical techniques that are most effective for the outcomes most closely related to the specific goals of the respective disciplinary clusters and the nature of the content to be taught. Unfortunately, most of what we know about effective pedagogical practices, given specific content areas within disciplines, is found in the volumes of research on effective teachers in elementary and secondary schools. (See the Stodolsky and Grossman and the Lenze chapters in this volume.) The research at the postsecondary level has tended to focus more on low-inference behaviors that cross disciplinary boundaries. Clearly, there is a strong need for discipline-specific research on pedagogical practice at the college and university level that goes beyond low-inference practices and considers the nature of the subject matter and disciplinary and institutional goals.

### References

Association of American Colleges, "Liberal Learning and the Arts and Sciences Major: The Challenge of Connecting Learning." Vol. 1. Washington, D.C.: Association of American Colleges, 1991a.

Association of American Colleges, "Liberal Learning and the Arts and Sciences Major: Reports from the Fields." Vol. 2. Washington, D.C.: Association of American Colleges, 1991b.

Biglan, A. "The Characteristics of Subject Matter in Different Academic Areas." *Journal of Applied Psychology,* 1973, 57 (3), 195–203.

Carnegie Foundation for the Advancement of Teaching. *A Classification of Institutions.* Princeton, N.J.: Carnegie Foundation for the Advancement of Teaching, 1987.

Lattuca, L. R., and Stark, J. S. "Will Disciplinary Perspectives Impede Curricular Reform?" *Journal of Higher Education,* 1994, 65 (3) 401–426.

Lattuca, L. R., and Stark, J. S. "Modifying the Major: Discretionary Thoughts from Ten Disciplines." *The Review of Higher Education,* 1995, *18,* 315–344.

McKeachie, W. J. "Student Ratings of Faculty: A Reprise." *Academe,* 1979, *65,* 384–397.

Murray, H. G. "Effective Teaching Behaviors in the College Classroom." In J. C. Smart (ed.), *Higher Education: Handbook of Theory and Research,* Vol. 7. New York: Agathon Press, 1991.

Smart, J. C., and Elton, C. F. "Goal Orientations of Academic Departments: A Test of Biglan's Model." *Journal of Applied Psychology,* 1975, *60,* 580–588.

Tom, F.K.T., and Cushman, H. R. "The Cornell Diagnostic Observation and Reporting System for Student Description of College Teaching." *Search,* 1975, *5,* 1–27.

*John C. Smart is professor of higher education in the College of Education at the University of Memphis.*

*Corinna A. Ethington is associate professor of educational research in the College of Education at the University of Memphis.*

*This chapter identifies academic disciplines that are more likely to embrace approaches instrumental to the improvement of undergraduate education.*

# Disciplines with an Affinity for the Improvement of Undergraduate Education

*John M. Braxton*

Variations among academic disciplines are significant and far-reaching (Braxton and Hargens, in press), involving a wide range of phenomena and matters of the disciplinary community, the university, the academic department, and the individual academic professional. At the level of the individual academic professional, variations among academic disciplines in different facets associated with teaching role performance are quite evident (Braxton and Hargens, in press). Such differences strongly suggest that individual faculty members, faculty developers, and academic affairs officers cannot generalize about teaching role performance in other disciplines from the limited perspective of their own academic discipline. Both faculty and administrators can improve their work through understanding how academic disciplines vary.

This chapter has two purposes: to summarize empirical research on aspects of teaching role performance in which disciplinary differences have been observed (teaching goals, teaching practices, course examination questions, and the relationship between teaching and research), and to present some implications of these disciplinary differences for the professional practice of college and university administrators in general and for efforts designed to improve undergraduate education in particular.

## Differences Between Hard and Soft Disciplines

The Biglan typology of academic disciplines (1973) and Lodahl and Gordon's (1972) notion of paradigmatic development are two analytical frameworks, with robust empirical support, for viewing variation among academic disciplines (Braxton and Hargens, in press). Common to both frameworks is the notion of the degree of paradigmatic development evident in an academic discipline. Biglan refers to this differentiating construct as the "hard-soft" dimension, whereas Lodahl and Gordon call it paradigmatic development. High and low paradigmatic development is interchangeable with Biglan's hard-soft dimension. Both Biglan and Lodahl and Gordon derive paradigmatic development from Kuhn's (1962, 1970) notion of the extent to which members of a discipline share beliefs about theory, methods, techniques, and pertinent problems for the discipline to pursue. Examples of hard paradigmatic disciplines are chemistry, physics, and biology, whereas political science, sociology, psychology, history, English, and economics are examples of disciplines exhibiting soft paradigmatic development. The distinction between disciplines exhibiting hard and soft paradigmatic development is used as an organizing framework for the research findings summarized below. (Although the studies reviewed may not have categorized the academic disciplines included as being either hard or soft, Biglan's typology was used to classify them as hard or soft.)

**Teaching Goals.** The importance attached to various teaching goals differs between disciplines of hard and soft paradigmatic development. Faculty in soft fields give greater importance to such goals as providing a broad general education and knowledge of oneself (Gaff and Wilson, 1971). Student character development is also more highly endorsed by faculty in soft fields (Smart and Elton, 1982). However, faculty in hard disciplines accord greater importance to student career preparation as a teaching goal (Gaff and Wilson, 1971).

The goals faculty espouse for academic majors also differ. Lattuca and Stark (1995) observe that hard disciplines emphasize cognitive concerns—learning of facts, principles, and concepts—whereas soft fields underscore these same goals but also attach importance to effective thinking skills such as critical thinking. These goals are registered in reports developed by faculty on the academic major, commissioned by the American Association of Colleges.

**Classroom Teaching Practices.** Course planning, approaches to teaching, pedagogical methods, and the use of scholarly based course activities vary between hard and soft disciplines. Stark, Lowther, Bentley, and Martens (1990) found that course planning by faculty tends to focus more on students—growth and development, preparation and needs—in soft disciplines than in hard fields. Consistent with their stress on effective thinking as the goal of the academic major, faculty in soft fields also tend to favor a more "discursive" approach to their classroom teaching than do their counterparts in hard fields. A discursive approach includes such faculty classroom behaviors as discussion of points of view other than one's own, discussion of issues beyond those covered in course readings, and the relating of course topics to other fields of study (Gaff and Wilson, 1971).

Pedagogical methods preferred in courses designed for undergraduate majors also vary between hard and soft fields. In comparison to soft fields, hard disciplines put more stress on student research experiences as a method for training undergraduate students in the discipline (Lattuca and Stark, 1995). Soft fields prefer an emphasis on oral and written communication skills, critical reading skills, and active learning as methods of pedagogy (Lattuca and Stark, 1995). In addition, faculty in soft disciplines are more likely to enact scholarly based course activities than their hard-discipline colleagues (Braxton, 1983). These scholarly based course activities, which fit Boyer's scholarship of teaching domain (1990), include lecturing on topics derived from current scholarly books, assigning research activities, and assigning current journal articles as required course reading.

**Student Assessment.** Disciplines vary in the kinds of examination questions faculty members use. Braxton and Nordvall (1988) observed that liberal arts college faculty in soft fields are more likely to ask examination questions requiring an analysis or synthesis of course content, whereas faculty in hard disciplines tend to ask more questions which require memorization and application of course material. Braxton (1993) confirmed a parallel pattern of questioning in research universities, with faculty in soft fields asking more questions which require critical thinking—analysis and synthesis—than do faculty in hard disciplines.

Hard and soft fields also differ in their attention to program review and student assessment. Lattuca and Stark (1995) observe that limited attention is paid to program review and student assessment by hard fields, whereas soft fields are more likely to view program review and student assessment as instruments for the improvement of teaching and learning (Lattuca and Stark, 1995).

**Relationship Between Teaching and Research.** An important issue is whether the roles of teaching and research complement or detract from one another (Faia, 1976; Fox, 1992). Complementarity is evident in soft fields, whereas neither complementarity nor conflict is apparent in hard disciplines. From a review of studies that examined the relationship between teaching performance and research productivity in various fields, Feldman (1987) found that teaching and research performance have a moderate ($r = .21$) relationship in soft disciplines, but an insignificant relationship ($r = .05$) in hard fields.

## Soft Fields as "Affinity Disciplines"

The differences between hard and soft disciplines summarized above suggest that efforts to improve undergraduate education are more likely to be successful in soft disciplines than in hard ones. Soft discipline faculty tend to value student character development, emphasize the development of critical thinking skills (analysis and synthesis), use discursive or student-centered teaching practices, and favor the use of program review and student assessment to improve teaching and learning. Thus, soft academic disciplines tend to have an affinity for embracing practices designed to improve college teaching whereas such efforts are not as likely to be successful in hard academic fields. As a result, I have labeled soft fields as "affinity disciplines," denoting their affinity for attention to the quality of teaching. The implications of the notion of affinity disciplines for faculty development and academic affairs administrators are discussed below.

**Implications for Faculty Development.** Weimer (1991) contends that the success of seminars and workshops depends on the presenter and the topic. The notion of affinity disciplines, however, is a mediating factor in the success of a faculty development workshop or seminar. Success or failure of workshops and seminars may hinge on whether the topics chosen match the teaching needs of hard and soft discipline faculty members. Faculty development officers may want to target some workshops or seminars for hard discipline faculty, whereas other workshops or seminars would be designed for soft discipline faculty. For example, a workshop or seminar focusing on lecturing skills would be more likely to meet the needs of hard discipline faculty, whereas one focusing on course activities which develop critical thinking skills would more likely match the needs of soft discipline faculty.

Faculty discussion groups should also be formulated with the distinctions between faculty in hard and soft disciplines in mind. Matching topics with the needs of faculty from hard and soft fields is important to the success of discussion groups.

**Implications for Academic Affairs Administrators.** Specific recommendations to improve undergraduate education often focus on improving undergraduate teaching through "student-centered" approaches (Chickering and Gamson, 1987; Katz, 1985). According to my analysis, affinity disciplines are more likely to implement such recommendations. Efforts to improve undergraduate education might thus be piloted in affinity disciplines before full implementation. If efforts falter in affinity disciplines, then failure in hard disciplines is also likely.

Academic program review and student outcomes assessment are among the primary activities of statewide boards of higher education (Hines, 1988), and they also are the concerns of academic administrators in many state-supported colleges and universities. Because affinity disciplines are more likely to use the findings of program review and student outcomes assessments, academic administrators may have to develop mechanisms for encouraging hard discipline departments to consider the implementation of recommendations derived from these assessments.

Academic administrators should recognize the distinctions between hard and soft academic disciplines in evaluating teaching for reappointment, promotion, and tenure. Although student course ratings may be common to the assessment of both groups of disciplines, other materials should be different. Because soft discipline faculty are more likely to take student needs into account in planning their courses, materials that manifest such concern should be provided. These materials might address such questions as: how is course content affected by student needs? How are course activities designed to address student needs? Soft discipline faculty are also more likely to emphasize critical thinking in their courses. Course examination questions and other materials that reflect the ways this emphasis is manifested in day-to-day course activities could also be provided to assess teaching of soft discipline faculty.

In conclusion, these implications for practice suggest both limitations and possibilities for faculty and administrative practice. These implications also suggest obstacles to college or universitywide change in teaching-related practices. Knowledge and understanding of such obstacles can build a foundation for change. Without that foundation, attempts to improve undergraduate education are likely to have only limited success.

## References

Biglan, A. "The Characteristics of Subject Matter in Different Academic Areas." *Journal of Applied Psychology,* 1973, *57* (3), 195–203.

Boyer, E. L. *Scholarship Reconsidered.* Princeton, N.J.: Carnegie Foundation for the Advancement of Teaching, 1990.

Braxton, J. M. "Teaching as Performance of Scholarly Based Course Activities: A Perspective on the Relationship Between Teaching and Research." *Review of Higher Education,* 1983, *7,* 21–33.

Braxton, J. M. "Selectivity and Rigor in Research Universities." *Journal of Higher Education,* 1993, *64,* 657–675.

Braxton, J. M., and Hargens, L. L. "Variation Among Academic Disciplines: Analytical Frameworks and Research." In J. C. Smart (ed.), *Higher Education: Handbook of Theory and Research.* New York: Agathon Press, in press.

Braxton, J. M., and Nordvall, R. C. "Quality of Graduate Department Origin of Faculty and Its Relationship to Undergraduate Course Examination Questions." *Research in Higher Education,* 1988, *28,* 145–159.

Chickering, A. W., and Gamson, Z. E. "Seven Principles for Good Practice in Undergraduate Education." *AAHE Bulletin,* 1987, *39,* 3–7.

Faia, M. A. "Teaching and Research: Rapport or Mesalliance." *Research in Higher Education,* 1976, *4,* 235–246.

Feldman, K. A. "Research Productivity and Scholarly Accomplishment of College Teachers as Related to Their Instructional Effectiveness: A Review and Exploration." *Research in Higher Education,* 1987, *26,* 227–298.

Fox, M. F. "Research, Teaching, and Publication Productivity: Mutuality Versus Competition in Academia." *Sociology of Education,* 1992, *65,* 293–305.

Gaff, J. G., and Wilson, R. C. "Faculty Cultures and Interdisciplinary Studies." *Journal of Higher Education,* 1971, *42,* 186–201.

Hines, E. R. *Higher Education and State Governments.* ASHE-ERIC Higher Education Report, no. 5. Washington, D.C.: Association for the Study of Higher Education, 1988.

Katz, J. "Teaching Based on Knowledge of Students." In J. Katz (ed.), *Teaching As Though Students Mattered.* New Directions for Teaching and Learning, no. 21. San Francisco: Jossey-Bass, 1985.

Kuhn, T. S. *The Structure of Scientific Revolutions.* Chicago: University of Chicago Press, 1970.

Lattuca, L. R., and Stark, J. S. "Modifying the Major: Discretionary Thoughts from Ten Disciplines." *Review of Higher Education,* 1995, *18* (3), 315–344.

Lodahl, J. B., and Gordon, G. G. "The Structure of Scientific Fields and the Functioning of University Graduate Departments." *American Sociological Review,* 1972, *37* (1), 57–72.

Smart, J. C., and Elton, C. F. "Validation of the Biglan Model." *Research in Higher Education,* 1982, *17,* 213–229.

Stark, J. S., Lowther, M. A., Bentley, R. J., and Martens, G. G. "Disciplinary Differences in Course Planning." *The Review of Higher Education,* 1990, *13,* 141–165.

Weimer, M. *Improving College Teaching.* San Francisco: Jossey-Bass, 1991.

*John M. Braxton is associate professor in the Department of Educational Leadership at Peabody College, Vanderbilt University.*

*Faculty's pedagogical knowledge centers on discipline-specific core issues that foster distinct ways of thinking about, talking about, and acting upon teaching.*

# Discipline-Specific Pedagogical Knowledge in Linguistics and Spanish

*Lisa Firing Lenze*

Researchers in higher education have paid little attention to faculty members' knowledge of teaching (Dunkin and Barnes, 1986) and even less to faculty's *discipline-specific* pedagogical knowledge. Only recently has research attention increased (see Beynon, Onslow, and Geddis, 1994; Irby, 1994; Lenze, 1995; and Quinlan, 1994). This gap in the literature should be filled, especially since researchers in secondary education persuasively argue that teachers' knowledge and beliefs about teaching are key to understanding teaching itself (Clark and Dunn, 1991; Clark and Peterson, 1986).

Given the discipline-specific context in which college faculty work (Becher, 1987), we are wise to investigate faculty's *discipline-specific* knowledge of teaching. Although there are no well-developed frameworks in higher education for thinking about teachers' knowledge (Dunkin and Barnes, 1986), research on teaching in secondary education does provide one framework that acknowledges disciplinary specialization in teaching. That is Shulman's (1986, 1987) notion of pedagogical content knowledge.

## Defining Pedagogical Content Knowledge

The concept of pedagogical content knowledge centers on the relationship between teachers' knowledge of the subject matter and teachers' practical pedagogical knowledge. In his early writings about pedagogical content knowledge, Shulman focused on teachers' representations of *content*, given their understandings about students' prior knowledge of the material. He wrote that pedagogical content knowledge includes "ways of representing and formulating the subject that make it comprehensible to others" (for example, analogies,

 65

illustrations, examples, and demonstrations) and "an understanding of . . . the conceptions and preconceptions that students of different ages and backgrounds bring with them" (Shulman, 1986, pp. 9–10).

Grossman's more recent definition (1990) describes four specific aspects of pedagogical content knowledge: (1) conceptions of the purposes for teaching a given subject matter, (2) knowledge of the instructional strategies useful for teaching a given content, (3) knowledge of students' understandings, and (4) knowledge of the curriculum.

## Four Cases of Pedagogical Content Knowledge

In order to better understand discipline-specific knowledge of teaching, I analyzed four cases of pedagogical content knowledge. Given my background and propensity for understanding teaching in Spanish and linguistics (eight years of Spanish study, along with experience advising foreign language pedagogy programs; and bachelor's and master's degrees in speech communication, a field that centers on language and communication), I selected two faculty hired in Spanish and two faculty hired in linguistics. I asked, "What is the nature of the pedagogical content knowledge of newly hired faculty in Spanish and linguistics who are relative novices to full-time college teaching?"

Data for this study came from the New Faculty Project, a research project of the National Center on Postsecondary Teaching, Learning, and Assessment. The four faculty in this study were hired in 1991 for their first full-time, tenure-track positions. They had relatively little pedagogical preparation and teaching experience. They agreed to intensive study during the fall academic term for each of three consecutive years. As I report results below, I rely mostly on interview data. Interview protocols for the first two years of this study focused on many facets of teaching; in the third year, protocols probed specifically for the four aspects of pedagogical content knowledge proposed by Grossman (1990) and mentioned above. (For a detailed explanation of analytical methods and findings across several data sources, see Lenze [1995].)

## What Distinguishes Teaching in Linguistics and Spanish

Using Grossman's (1990) conceptualization of pedagogical content knowledge as a guiding framework, I found in each discipline a core concept around which knowledge of teaching revolved. A core concept is an idea, appearing throughout the data, that connects and underlies almost all the data in a given case. In each discipline, the two faculty shared a distinguishing core concept on which their knowledge of teaching centered. For linguistics faculty the core concept was argumentation, and for Spanish faculty it was production. These concepts pervaded the four aspects of pedagogical content knowledge mentioned by Grossman (1990).

## Linguistics

**Argumentation: The Core Concept.** To Maxene and Margaret, the two linguistics faculty, argumentation meant connecting observations with theory and then supporting, advancing, or refuting theory. They agreed that argumentation was necessary to help students appreciate the complexity of language.

*Conceptions of Purposes.* Argumentation clearly emerged in the linguistics faculty members' expressions of their purposes for teaching linguistics. They wanted to get students to argue, to think analytically, to see things from a linguist's perspective. Of the two linguistics faculty, Margaret explained the role of argumentation more clearly: "One of the main things they're supposed to be learning, according to me, is syntactic argumentation. How you argue for a particular position. . . . What often happens is in doing exercises, somebody will offer their hypothesis about what the answer is. Somebody else will say, "No, it can't be that because . . ." and they'll give a piece of evidence. That, I really like."

*Knowledge of Instructional Strategies.* The two linguistics faculty wanted students to argue in class. In their courses, representative strategies ranged from discrete student activities, such as frequent breaks in lecture for students' examples and counterexamples and occasional small group tasks (in which students were to engage in critical argumentation about the text), to more pervasive teacher activities centered on modeling argumentation.

*Knowledge of Students' Understandings.* Maxene and Margaret said they knew that students struggled with, among other things, argumentation and thinking like a linguist. Maxene explained, "I think that the thing they struggle with is not the facts and figures. . . . It's the return to 'And how does this bear on human language development and the questions we're asking there, like nature versus nurture?' That's really hard." Both Maxene and Margaret maintained that making arguments was something to wrestle with in order to understand language.

*Knowledge of Curriculum.* Maxene and Margaret elaborated least on their knowledge of curriculum. Still, evidence of argumentation emerged at least in Maxene's curricular knowledge. Maxene, whose research interests were somewhat related to the courses she taught, relied on her own knowledge of arguments in her specific subfield to guide her through the curriculum. Her course was logically organized by empirically based arguments in the subfield of language development. Thus, for Maxene, argument provided order to an otherwise loose, unorganized curriculum.

## Spanish

**Production: The Core Concept.** Whereas linguistics faculty's knowledge centered on argumentation, Spanish faculty members' knowledge was characterized by a core concept of production. Sometimes called "usage," "practice," or "speaking in Spanish," production was like participation—but something more than participation. It was participation *in the spoken language of Spanish.*

*Conceptions of Purposes.* The Spanish faculty members' conceptions of the purposes for teaching Spanish differed from one another, but each contained the idea of production. Juanita's purpose was to teach students to produce Spanish, but to do so in a *practical* sense. She wanted students to learn the Spanish they would read in newspaper articles and use on the street.

Rachael, on the other hand, wanted students to engage in a long-term relationship with Spanish. Her biggest wish was to get students producing, enjoying, and wanting to continue: "Not that they do it because it's a requisite or a prerequisite, you know? I know there's a little bit of a devilish instinct inside of me to get them really involved. . . . I want them to keep on going."

*Knowledge of Instructional Strategies.* The two Spanish faculty viewed production as integral to learning and adopted interactive strategies as the central mechanism for teaching their course content. Participatory strategies were not *placed within* lectures; they *constituted* the whole class period. Representative activities included drilling, discussion, question and answer exercises, and pair work. Rachael summarized that to teach Spanish, "I gotta rely on using, producing it." Juanita echoed that Spanish is "just something that you learn through use. Just constant use."

*Knowledge of Students' Understandings.* Juanita and Rachael knew of two difficulties related to production. They knew of affective barriers to production (for example, fear of speaking, shyness, and attitudes of arrogance), and they knew that students' understandings of languages *other than* Spanish (primarily English) influenced (sometimes positively and sometimes negatively) students' production of Spanish. Most impressive was their consensus that the best way to overcome these difficulties was to produce more. Juanita said, "To overcome difficulties in Spanish, students just need to do lots of practice." Rachael echoed, "Those who participate [in Spanish] really do improve, and those who don't, don't get better."

*Knowledge of Curriculum.* Like the linguistics teachers, Juanita and Rachael elaborated least on their knowledge of curriculum. Still, evidence of production emerged at least in Rachael's curricular knowledge. Her global view of the curriculum (compared to Juanita's fine-tuned perspective) focused on a set of structural achievements to be attained in language production. That is, rather than focus on each lesson with a particular set of vocabulary words to be learned, Rachael saw the curriculum as words, then phrases, then sentences, and finally complete thoughts to be produced.

## Conclusions About Discipline-Based Knowledge of Teaching

From this examination of new faculty members' pedagogical content knowledge and from my inquiry as to how faculty developed this knowledge, I reached four conclusions about discipline-specific knowledge of teaching and its development. These conclusions suggest implications for researchers, administrators, faculty developers, and faculty.

First, two core disciplinary concepts pulled together much of faculty's knowledge of teaching: argumentation in linguistics and production in Spanish. These central concepts fostered distinct ways of thinking about, talking about, and acting upon teaching. For example, the concept of production centered on action, and thus Juanita and Rachael were predisposed to develop knowledge of instructional strategies to move students toward participation. On the other hand, the concept of argumentation in linguistics centered on logic and theory. Given their students' *lack* of knowledge about empirical, analytical, and theoretical ideas, Maxene and Margaret were predisposed to focus on knowledge of students' preconceptions and misunderstandings. Thus, faculty in the two disciplines developed knowledge of equally important but quite different aspects of teaching.

Those who aim to *improve* teaching should take note of what faculty in different disciplines know and do not know about teaching in their fields. Here lie the seeds for pedagogical development and improvement. Furthermore, researchers aiming to *understand* college teaching must discover what faculty hold as the core concept of teaching in different fields. These concepts are key to understanding why faculty in different fields teach as they do.

Second, although faculty relied on several sources for the development of pedagogical content knowledge (for example, past model teachers, department colleagues, and reflection on experiences as students and teachers), what seemed to make the most difference in discipline-specific knowledge over three years was direct teaching experience in several different courses. If it is direct contact with the subject matter and those who know about the subject matter that helps develop knowledge of teaching, then administrators should assign release time to new faculty for teaching, just as they assign release time for research.

During such "teaching semesters," faculty should be paired with senior faculty to team teach no more than two courses at a time. The team-teaching experience would be enhanced by reflective groups centered on developing knowledge about specific courses. Without administrative support for such activities, teaching knowledge (along with teaching efficiency and expertise) will continue to develop slowly and sporadically.

Third, a good deal of discipline-specific knowledge of teaching was implicit but accessible when a reflective observer helped faculty uncover what was tacit. For example, when I first reflected back to the linguistics faculty their idea of argumentation, neither understood why I was so "preoccupied" with it. After further reflection, both agreed that "seeing things like a linguist" (that is, from a perspective of argumentation) accurately portrayed one of their underlying goals in teaching.

Faculty developers are in a good position to assist faculty in reflecting on their teaching and in making the tacit conscious. They are unbiased observers, trained consultants, and reflective listeners—a natural choice when looking for someone to work with small groups of new faculty focused on developing teaching knowledge. Joint-authored pieces of research on discipline-specific teaching could even result. Both faculty and faculty developers would benefit from such associations.

Fourth, within disciplines, discipline-specific pedagogical knowledge developed in differing amounts. For example, Maxene knew more than Margaret about engaging students in effective instructional strategies in their field. Rachael knew more than Juanita about students' affective barriers to producing Spanish. Thus, new faculty can benefit from sharing knowledge with each other. Separately, new faculty have not yet developed a great deal of knowledge; but together, they know quite a bit.

## References

Becher, T. "The Disciplinary Shaping of the Profession." In B. R. Clark (ed.), *The Academic Profession.* Berkeley: University of California Press, 1987.

Beynon, C., Onslow, B., and Geddis, A. "Learning About Teaching in Teacher Education: The Role of Curricular Saliency." Paper presented at the American Educational Research Association Conference, New Orleans, April 1994.

Clark, C. M., and Dunn, S. "Second-Generation Research on Teachers' Planning, Intentions, and Routines." In H. C. Waxman and H. J. Walberg (eds.), *Effective Teaching: Current Research.* Berkeley: McCutchan, 1991.

Clark, C. M., and Peterson, P. L. "Teachers' Thought Processes." In M. C. Wittrock (ed.), *Handbook of Research on Teaching,* 3rd ed. New York: Macmillan, 1986.

Dunkin, M. J., and Barnes, J. "Research on Teaching in Higher Education." In M. C. Wittrock (ed.), *Handbook of Research on Teaching,* 3rd ed. New York: Macmillan, 1986.

Grossman, P. L. *The Making of a Teacher: Teacher Knowledge and Teacher Education.* New York: Teachers College Press, 1990.

Irby, D. M. "What Clinical Teachers in Medicine Need to Know." *Academic Medicine,* 1994, 69 (5), 333–342.

Lenze, L. F. "The Pedagogical Content Knowledge of Faculty Relatively New to College Teaching." Unpublished doctoral dissertation, Educational Processes Program, Northwestern University, 1995.

Quinlan, K. M. "Uncovering Discipline-Specific Interpretations of the 'Scholarship of Teaching': Peer Review and Faculty Perceptions of Scholarly Teaching." Paper presented at the Association for the Study of Higher Education Conference, Tucson, November 1994.

Shulman, L. S. "Those Who Understand: Knowledge Growth in Teaching." *Educational Researcher,* 1986, 15 (2), 4–14.

Shulman, L. S. "Knowledge and Teaching: Foundations of the New Reform." *Harvard Educational Review,* 1987, 57 (1), 1–22.

*Lisa Firing Lenze recently received her doctorate from the School of Education and Social Policy at Northwestern University. She is the co-editor of* Learning from Students: Early-Term Student Feedback in Higher Education *(National Center on Teaching, Learning, and Assessment, 1994).*

*A study of the role of subject matter in shaping high school teachers' beliefs, curricular concerns, and instructional practices complements studies of the disciplines in higher education and suggests implications for research and practice.*

# Subject-Matter Differences in Secondary Schools: Connections to Higher Education

*Susan S. Stodolsky, Pamela L. Grossman*

In this chapter, we describe our research on subject matter as a context for high school teachers and discuss the study's implications for higher education.

Though high school subjects are derived from university disciplines, for both historical and pedagogical reasons (see, for example, Goodson, 1985), school subjects differ significantly from the traditional disciplines (Grossman and Stodolsky, 1994). The same department may offer courses with a number of disciplinary origins, and teachers in these departments may represent a variety of disciplinary backgrounds. For example, social studies teachers may be trained in such different disciplines as psychology, history, political science, economics, sociology, or even geography. In contrast, mathematics teachers tend to share a common college background with courses in calculus, algebra, and so on. Thus, the scope, or relative breadth, of school subjects, may have implications for curricular coordination, collaboration, and teachers' conceptions of subject matter.

Since teaching is the primary concern of high school teachers, our investigation centers on the issues of teaching, curriculum and instruction, and collegial relations.

This research was supported by the Spencer Foundation and the University of Chicago School Mathematics Research Fund. We appreciate their generous support, but we retain all responsibility for statements made.

We acknowledge the very helpful research and editorial assistance provided by Cheryl Littman at the University of Chicago.

## A Study of Teachers in Five Academic Subjects

Our research investigates how subject matter forms a context for high school teachers' work. We surveyed 399 English, math, science, social studies, and foreign language teachers from sixteen high schools in California and Michigan and conducted twelve case studies of math and English teachers in three high schools. We also analyzed interviews collected by our colleagues with teachers at the sixteen schools. (Full details on the sample can be found in Stodolsky and Grossman, 1995, and McLaughlin and Talbert, 1993.) Among other questions, we asked: how do teachers conceive of the subject matter they teach? What goals do teachers espouse for their teaching? What beliefs do teachers hold regarding student learning and student ability? What instructional approaches do teachers use? What constrains teachers of different subjects with respect to what they can teach?

In our surveys we asked teachers to describe the subjects they taught in terms of three salient characteristics. The *Defined* scale captures the extent to which teachers believe the subject is composed of an agreed upon, well-defined body of knowledge and skills. The *Dynamic* scale captures beliefs about whether knowledge in the subject is changing rapidly or is relatively static. The *Sequential* scale assesses the extent to which teachers think knowledge in the subject is ordered with respect to the presentation or acquisition of topics. In case study interviews, we probed more deeply into the specific conceptions of subject matter held by individual math and English teachers and the relationships among their beliefs, their curriculum, and their instructional practices.

**Conceptions of Subject Matter.** Table 8.1 shows the mean scores and results of an analysis of variance for teachers of five academic subjects on the three scales measuring teachers' conceptions of their subject matter.

Survey responses verified that teachers in the five academic subjects view their school subjects differently. While all teachers see their subject as Defined, math and foreign language teachers agree more strongly than teachers of English, social studies, or science that their subjects are clearly defined. The Dynamic scale sharply separates teachers of different subjects. English teachers most strongly view the knowledge in their field as changing, while math teachers tend to see their subject as less dynamic and more cut-and-dry. And finally, math and foreign language teachers view their subject as Sequential, while English, social studies, and science teachers see their subjects as only slightly sequential.

The surveys show that teachers in a subject area operate within a somewhat unique conceptual context regarding their school subject. Individual teachers may diverge, however, from the normative view that characterizes their subject area. For example, in our case studies, we found a number of points of comparison and contrast between two highly experienced math teachers, Yvonne and Carolyn. When asked to describe mathematics as a field of study, they answered rather similarly. Yvonne described math "as a way of life. It is

## Table 8.1. Mean Responses to Conceptions of Subject-Matter Scales for Teachers of Academic Subjects and ANOVA Results

| Scale[1] | Mathematics (n = 82) | | Foreign Language (n = 42) | | Science (n = 81) | | English (n = 109) | | Social Studies (n = 85) | | Subject Effect | |
|---|---|---|---|---|---|---|---|---|---|---|---|---|
| | Mean[2] | SD | Mean | SD | Mean | SD | Mean | SD | Mean | SD | F | p < |
| Defined | 4.92[a] | 0.73 | 4.89[a] | 0.75 | 4.57[b] | 0.90 | 4.34[b] | 0.82 | 4.36[b] | 0.91 | 7.96 | .0001 |
| Dynamic | 3.65[d] | 0.88 | 4.07[c] | 0.99 | 4.70[b] | 0.82 | 4.99[a] | 0.75 | 4.64[b] | 0.99 | 31.65 | .0001 |
| Sequential | 4.92[a] | 0.73 | 4.96[a] | 0.95 | 3.99[b] | 0.90 | 4.01[b] | 1.15 | 3.68[b] | 0.97 | 25.74 | .0001 |

[1]Maximum scale score is 6.

[2]Alphabetic superscripts show results of Duncan's multiple range test. Each letter identifies members of a cluster significantly different from those with another letter.

inherent in almost everything we do. . . . You can live your life using *things* that are taught in math—ideas, concepts, methods of attack—without actually being mathematical." In a similar vein, Carolyn, who taught in the same district, described mathematics as a process of analytical thinking. Carolyn said, "I think of it as a way of people being able to think through things completely and to look at all options and not just be locked into one way of solving things."

But despite the similarity of their general statements about math, Yvonne and Carolyn diverged about specific aspects of math and teaching math. Yvonne saw math as only slightly sequential or defined; she believed students could be taught topics even if they had not previously mastered skills others would claim were prerequisite. For example, she explained that by providing a calculator to a student who had not mastered arithmetic operations, the student could go on to algebra instead of going over material with which he or she had been repeatedly unsuccessful. In contrast, Carolyn saw math as very defined and highly sequential and held a mastery view of the subject, "because with math, if they don't get the basics at the very beginning, it just mushrooms on them. So as they get further and further along, they get more and more lost." Carolyn would not permit her students to use calculators until they could demonstrate adequate mastery of arithmetic operations. Carolyn's highly sequential view of math also evidenced itself in her very strong commitment to a placement program based on prior student achievement. Yvonne, on the other hand, preferred not to know how students performed prior to taking her courses.

Two English teachers in the same district, Yori and Ian, also showed strong contrasts in their conceptions of the subject matter. Yori's definition of English was very broad and multifaceted, including vocabulary, language, grammar, composition, literature, reading, and speaking. He described teaching English as "trying to juggle all [these parts] and keep everything going, and that's difficult." For Ian, on the other hand, English is a body of knowledge students have to learn in order to be culturally literate—a common body of knowledge contained in the world of classic literature (the canon).

**Curriculum and Instruction.** We were particularly interested in the extent to which different subjects pose constraints or opportunities in the area of curriculum. How much freedom do high school teachers have in determining what they teach and what curricular materials they use, and does this vary in different school subjects? Elsewhere (Stodolsky and Grossman, 1995), we have shown that teaching a defined and sequential subject is associated with less control over what is taught and more coordination with colleagues.

The present survey shows that math teachers, compared to teachers in other fields, report significantly less control over what they teach and more standardization of curriculum in terms of common exams and common content. As one math teacher said, "The outline of the topics you can't change too much, because so much of algebra depends on what you do previously. You can't do a lot of problem solving until you've had positive and negative numbers." Math teachers also report more coordination of the curriculum with other math teachers and more rotation of courses than teachers in other fields, especially science and social studies, which are each composed of a number of disciplines. Math and foreign language teachers, both representing sequential areas, report more pressure to cover the content in their curriculum.

English teachers, on the other hand, report considerable autonomy in choice of content and a lack of standardization in the curriculum. One teacher explained the many different ways English competence could be developed: "My goal is to have a student read. If they are going to read a fantasy book—and I don't like fantasy—that's OK. They're reading." Yori, one of our case study English teachers, explained that he had changed his approach to teaching writing and literature in order to be more effective with a changing student body. In the case of writing, he shifted from expository writing to personal response writing. In literature, Yori abandoned a chronological, text-driven approach for a more thematically organized curriculum. He commented that with the new approach, "we can try to find literature that appeals to [kids] that addresses concerns they would have as adolescents, and to steer them in ways we believe are sound as far as values. . . . What we choose for the kids to read is extremely important, and if you try to impose upon them . . . works which are too far removed from their personal world . . . you're fighting a losing battle." The relatively permissive (Protherough and Atkinson, 1992) or nonhierarchical nature of English seems to make it easier for teachers such as Yori to have autonomy in selecting topics and materials for instruction. In fact, English teachers report that their departments have explicit policies that grant autonomy to teachers with respect to what they teach.

Although English as a subject allows teachers more flexibility in what they teach than do other subjects such as math, the extent to which teachers take advantage of this flexibility depends in part on their individual beliefs about the subject matter. For example, Yori's district colleague Ian wanted his students "to be acquainted with the world of literature and then, I hope, not remain a stranger to good writing." Though Ian's English department granted teachers autonomy in selecting what to teach, Ian felt he should not alter the texts used in his courses because of his personal view of English as a particular body of knowledge to be learned. Even though Ian, like Yori, faced a change of student body, he did not alter his instructional program or curriculum and experienced much frustration in dealing with a changing student population.

Another important curricular issue concerns how the curriculum is arranged for students of varying abilities. We found that math and science teachers in our sample more strongly endorsed student differentiation or tracking. In the case of math, the belief in tracking may be partly a function of concern for proper placement in a sequential subject. However, the response may also reflect belief in the role of ability in learning math and science. Perhaps based on concerns for social justice, social studies teachers very strongly reject tracking.

In addition to differentiating the curriculum to respond to a range of students, teachers may also adjust grading, assessment, and instructional practices. The basis for grading reported by teachers in our sample differs depending on the subject they teach. All teachers base some portion of grades on effort and participation, but foreign language, English, and social studies teachers put more weight on effort in awarding grades than do science and math teachers; the latter place more emphasis on absolute levels of achievement.

According to teachers' survey responses, individualization, in which students have some choice of assignments as well as opportunities to revise and redo assignments, is another aspect of instruction that shows subject-matter differences. English teachers endorse individualization in instruction significantly more than math and science teachers.

To understand a particular teacher's practices requires knowing how the teacher views the subject, the students, and the goals. But it also requires knowledge of the context in which the teacher works (school, department, nature of the student body). To return to the math teachers, Yvonne and Carolyn, the departments in which each worked supported their individual beliefs and perhaps helped create their different responses to the use of calculators and other changes in instruction. The math department at Esperanza, in which Yvonne taught, strongly supported new approaches to math teaching to help improve student learning. In comparison, the Rancho department of which Carolyn was a member resisted innovation, holding firmly to a position of strict student placement through a testing program created by the department. The availability of resources may also influence the choice of curriculum. High school teachers are ultimately constrained by what is in the book room or what other curriculum resources are available.

## Research Agenda and Implications for Higher Education

The interconnections between secondary schools and colleges and universities are strong and symbiotic. High school teachers prepare students for higher education; these teachers, in turn, have received both subject matter and pedagogical preparation from faculties in higher education. What does our study suggest about issues for further research and implications for higher education?

The "hard-soft" distinction (Biglan, 1973) made with respect to academic disciplines seems to resonate in secondary schools. Math and science teachers, having been trained in hard disciplines, exhibit various practices consistent with the existence of a major paradigm and a consensus about knowledge verification in their fields. (For a specific discussion of disciplinary differences in knowledge verification processes in higher education, see the Donald chapter in this volume.) Their adherence to absolute achievement standards in grading is an example, as is their reluctance to grant students much choice in their assignments or tasks. Other commonalities between math and science teachers, however, may result more directly from features of their socialization into these disciplines in college (we realize that the broader culture, too, conveys ideas about the higher status of science and math and emphasizes ability as a key to success).

*Sequence* is a feature of disciplines not usually discussed in the higher education literature. Our findings regarding math and foreign language teaching in high schools suggest that perceived sequence plays an important role in determining whether there is flexibility in the content of courses and whether prerequisites are established. It also suggests that department members in fields believed to be sequential may be more likely to work together to ensure appropriate instructional coverage. In some respects, instructional coordination may be an analog to collaboration or consultation on research and could be profitably investigated.

High school English and social studies teachers seem to endorse a broader range of instructional practices and goals than math and science teachers do. As soft fields with broad scope, English and social studies appear to permit multiple definitions of the area in terms of course content. Teachers of English and social studies experience autonomy in planning curricula and incorporate more instructional approaches that permit student choice and allow for student interactions. What kind of instructional approaches occur in these disciplines in universities? How varied are curricular offerings, even under the same course titles? What kind of prerequisite structures occur in English and social science departments?

Beliefs about subject matter formed during higher education are critically important for prospective teachers, as current research demonstrates the power of teachers' beliefs about the subject they teach and the difficulty of changing them (Cohen, 1991). Because prospective secondary teachers take the bulk of their coursework in arts and sciences classes, faculty in higher education serve as de facto teacher educators. In arts and sciences classes, prospective teachers not only acquire subject matter knowledge, but they also develop beliefs about the nature of the subject and also serve an "apprenticeship of observation" in how the subject is taught (Lortie, 1975). Grossman (1990), for example, illustrated that beginning high school English teachers modeled their instruction on their recent experiences in college.

Given the importance of undergraduate learning for prospective teachers, future research might investigate the "hidden curriculum" of higher education. For example, do prospective math teachers come to believe that higher mathematics is not for everyone, from a college curriculum designed to weed out all but the most able math students? Do prospective science teachers develop an elite view of their field through the way in which science offerings are structured in universities? Similarly, do beliefs about the importance of sequence in learning a subject reflect the ways in which the disciplinary curriculum is structured in higher education?

College faculty need to be more mindful of the curricular and instructional models they provide for students, as the college students of today will become the teachers and professors of the future. An awareness of their role as instructional exemplars might also motivate faculty to improve teaching in colleges and universities for all students, as well as enhancing the perceived importance of teaching in higher education.

## References

Biglan, A. "The Characteristics of Subject Matter in Different Academic Areas." *Journal of Applied Psychology*, 1973, 57(3), 195–203.

Cohen, D. K. "A Revolution in One Classroom: The Case of Mrs. Oublier." *Educational Evaluation and Policy Analysis,* 1991, *12,* 311–330.

Goodson, I. F. (ed.). *Social Histories of the Secondary Curriculum.* London: Falmer Press, 1985.

Grossman, P. L. *The Making of a Teacher: Teacher Knowledge and Teacher Education.* New York: Teachers College Press, 1990.

Grossman, P. L., and Stodolsky, S. S. "Considerations of Content and the Circumstances of Secondary School Teaching." In L. Darling-Hammond (ed.), *Review of Research in Education,* Vol. 20. Washington, D.C.: American Educational Research Association, 1994.

Lortie, D. C. *Schoolteacher: A Sociological Study.* Chicago: University of Chicago Press, 1975.

McLaughlin, M. W., and Talbert, J. E. *Contexts that Matter for Teaching and Learning: Strategic Opportunities for Meeting the Nation's Educational Goals.* Stanford, Calif.: Center for Research on the Context of Secondary School Teaching, Stanford University, 1993.

Protherough, R., and Atkinson, J. "How English Teachers See English Teaching." *Research in the Teaching of English,* 1992, *26,* 385–407.

Stodolsky, S. S., and Grossman, P. L. "The Impact of Subject Matter on Curricular Activity: An Analysis of Five Academic Subjects." *American Educational Research Journal,* 1995, *32* (2), 227–249.

*Susan S. Stodolsky is professor of education and of psychology at the University of Chicago.*

*Pamela L. Grossman is associate professor of curriculum and instruction in the College of Education, University of Washington.*

# PART THREE

Disciplinary Differences
in Students' Attitudes and
Perceptions of Their Teachers
and Their Learning

*Although students rate different academic fields differently, the Biglan clusters seem not to explain these differences.*

# Disciplinary Differences in What Is Taught and in Students' Perceptions of What They Learn and of How They Are Taught

*William E. Cashin, Ronald G. Downey*

In one of his early reviews of the research on student ratings of teaching, Feldman (1978) suggested that students rated different academic disciplines differently. He concluded that students' ratings of courses in English, humanities, arts, and language tend to be higher than ratings in the social sciences (especially political science, sociology, psychology, and economics courses); and these in turn receive higher ratings than science (excepting certain subareas of the biological sciences), mathematics, and engineering courses.

An early analysis of data from the IDEA (Instructional Development and Effectiveness Assessment) system also revealed differences in student ratings of different disciplines (Cashin, Noma, and Hanna, 1987). (IDEA is a system of student ratings of instruction and courses; since 1975 it has been used by over 450 colleges and universities ranging from two-year institutions to research universities.) Cashin and Clegg (1987) explored whether the differences reported in the IDEA data might be contaminated by sampling errors introduced by the *specific* institutions that had used IDEA. However, even after controlling for different institutional characteristics, significant differences remained among academic disciplines.

Pursuing the question further, Cashin (1990) analyzed data from the Educational Testing Service's Student Instructional Report (Educational Testing Service, 1982a, 1982b), as well as from IDEA. The differences in the ratings of academic disciplines in the two systems were both clear and very similar to those first reported by Feldman. Cashin suggested six variables that might be

NEW DIRECTIONS FOR TEACHING AND LEARNING, no. 64, Winter 1995 © Jossey-Bass Publishers related to these differences in ratings: the degree of quantification (math) required by the course, whether the course was part of a sequence, how specifiable and masterable the course was (how much agreement there was on the limits of what was to be learned), differences in students from various majors, whether a course was used to screen out students, and finally, whether some courses/fields might actually be more poorly taught (and therefore deserve lower ratings). He concluded that *multiple* causes were probably operating.

Four other studies conducted at individual institutions have explored variations in student ratings across different academic disciplines (Barnes and Barnes, 1993; Franklin and Theall, 1992; Neumann and Neumann, 1983; Smith and Cranton, 1992). Each found significant differences but no clear explanations for them. This growing body of research is in the stage of identifying and describing the differences, but it is still not clear why the differences occur. Biglan's (1973a, 1973b) clustering of academic disciplines offers one approach to studying why differences across academic fields are found.

## Biglan's Clusters

Biglan (1973a, 1973b) suggested that academic disciplines differed along three dimensions: hard (disciplines that work from an agreed-upon paradigm) versus soft, pure (basic research) versus applied, and nonlife (disciplines that study inanimate objects) versus life. Applying Biglan's three dimensions results in eight different clusters. For example, astronomy, chemistry, geology, mathematics, and physics are all examples of hard, pure, nonlife disciplines.

To test whether Biglan's clusters can explain the differences in student ratings across academic disciplines, we used data from eight academic fields—of the forty-four available—from the IDEA system's data base of 101,710 classes (Sixbury and Cashin, 1995b). The eight fields represent each of Biglan's eight clusters, as follows: mathematics (hard, pure, nonlife; 5,150 classes in our sample); computer and information study (hard, applied, nonlife, 2,777); biological science (hard, pure, life, 3,455); agriculture and natural resources (hard, applied, life, 725); English language and literature (soft, pure, nonlife, 8,013); accounting (soft, applied, nonlife, 2,906); psychology (soft, pure, life, 3,855); and education (soft, applied, life, 8,319).

## Three Approaches to the Data

The IDEA system differs from many systems of student ratings of instructors and courses in some important ways. First, its primary measure of teaching effectiveness is self-reported student learning rather than teacher behavior. Thus, students rate the progress they have made on ten general course objectives, items 21–30 (see Table 9.1 for the wording of each IDEA item). For example, item 21 is "Gaining factual knowledge (terminology, classifications, methods, trends)." Second, the IDEA system has the faculty member weight the importance of each of the ten course objectives for that particular course on a Faculty Information Form (FIF) using a three-point scale: 3 = an essential objective, 2 = an important objective, and 1 = an objective of no more than minor importance. The first section of Table 9.1 (FIF 1–10) gives the average faculty weightings of items 21–30; for example, FIF 1 is the importance weighting for item 21, and so on. These weights are used in the computer analysis (which gives zero weight to objectives of minor importance) of the students' ratings of their progress on each item. By using these weightings, IDEA becomes a flexible system for evaluation and improvement. Different courses have different instructional goals; therefore different teaching methods are appropriate. If the students report that they learned what the instructor said he or she was trying to teach, it suggests that the instruction was effective. Cohen (1981) and Feldman (1989), in reviews of the research from multisection validity studies, both concluded that there was a significant positive relationship between items asking students how much they had learned and their scores on an external exam, developed by people other than the instructors. Finally, IDEA contains the traditional items, for example 1 through 20, related to teachers' behaviors in the classroom.

In this study we use the instructor's weightings of the importance of the ten course objectives (FIF 1–10) to discuss "what is taught"; we use the students' reports of their progress on the corresponding items (21–30) to discuss "what is learned" and IDEA items dealing with teacher behavior (items 1–20) to discuss "how they are taught."

**What Is Taught.** Table 9.1 shows the means for the ten FIF weightings (which use a 3-point scale) and for the 38 IDEA items (which use a 5-point scale) for the entire data base (101,710 classes from 133 colleges and universities; see Sixbury and Cashin, 1995b, for details). For the eight academic fields, however, *differences* rather than means are shown (the mean for the entire data base was subtracted from the mean for that field). Using differences makes it easier to see whether a given field tends to be rated higher or lower than the entire data base. For example, the mean for the entire data base on FIF 1 (which corresponds to item 21, gaining factual knowledge) is 2.2; the difference for mathematics/statistics is +.3. So the mean for mathematics/statistics was 2.5 (on this 3-point scale, where a mean of 3.0 would indicate that the objective was weighted as essential for *all* of the classes). On average, having the students gain factual knowledge was weighted as more important for the 5,150 mathematics/statistics classes than it was for the classes in the total data base.

The most highly weighted objectives across the entire data base, were FIF 1 and FIF 2 (gaining factual knowledge, item 21; and learning fundamental principles and theories, item 22). What this suggests—at least as reflected in these one hundred thousand classes—is that U.S. higher education is still emphasizing teaching at the two lowest levels of Bloom's cognitive taxonomy (Bloom and others, 1956), emphasizing memorization with some paraphrasing. This does not mean that the higher levels of the taxonomy are ignored; FIF 3 and FIF 4—dealing with application, analysis, synthesis, and evaluation— are the next most heavily weighted objectives. More to the point, if we look at

## Table 9.1. IDEA Item Means Difference for Eight Academic Fields

| | Entire Database 101710 | Math/ Statistics 5150 | Comp. & Info. Study 2777 | Biological Science 3455 | Ag. & Nat. Resources 725 | English Lang./Lit. 8013 | Accounting 2906 | Psychology 3855 | Education 8319 |
|---|---|---|---|---|---|---|---|---|---|
| N | | | | | | | | | |
| | *Faculty Weightings of Importance* | | | | | | | | |
| FIF 1. Gaining factual knowledge (terminology, classifications, methods, trends). | 2.2 | +.3 | +.3 | +.5 | +.3 | −.7 | +.4 | +.2 | 0.0 |
| FIF 2. Learning fundamental principles, generalizations, or theories. | 2.2 | +.2 | +.1 | +.3 | +.1 | −.5 | +.4 | +.2 | 0.0 |
| FIF 3. Learning to apply course material to improve rational thinking, problem-solving, and decision making. | 2.0 | +.2 | 0.0 | −.3 | +.1 | −.3 | 0.0 | −.2 | +.1 |
| FIF 4. Developing specific skills, competencies, and points of view needed by professionals in the field most closely related to this course. | 1.8 | −.2 | +.2 | −.2 | +.3 | −.4 | +.2 | −.2 | +.5 |
| FIF 5. Learning how professionals in this field go about the process of gaining new knowledge. | 1.4 | −.3 | −.1 | 0.0 | 0.0 | −.2 | −.1 | +.2 | +.1 |
| FIF 6. Developing creative capacities. | 1.4 | −.2 | −.1 | −.3 | −.1 | +.3 | −.3 | −.2 | 0.0 |
| FIF 7. Developing a sense of personal responsibility (self-reliance, self-discipline). | 1.5 | −.2 | −.2 | −.1 | 0.0 | 0.0 | −.2 | −.1 | +.1 |
| FIF 8. Gaining a broader understanding and appreciation of intellectual-cultural activity (music, science, literature, etc.). | 1.3 | −.2 | −.2 | 0.0 | −.2 | +.5 | −.2 | −.1 | −.1 |
| FIF 9. Developing skill in expressing myself orally or in writing. | 1.6 | −.5 | −.4 | −.4 | −.3 | +1.0 | −.4 | −.2 | −.1 |
| FIF 10. Discovering the implications of the course material for understanding myself (interests, talents, values, etc.). | 1.4 | −.3 | −.2 | −.2 | −.2 | +.2 | −.3 | +.4 | +.1 |

## Students' Reports of Progress

|  | | | | | | | | | | |
|---|---|---|---|---|---|---|---|---|---|---|
| 21. | Gaining factual knowledge (terminology, classifications, methods, trends). | 3.8 | −.1 | −.1 | +.2 | +.2 | −.3 | 0.0 | 0.0 | +.1 |
| 22. | Learning fundamental principles, generalizations, or theories. | 3.8 | 0.0 | −.2 | 0.0 | 0.0 | −.3 | 0.0 | +.1 | +.1 |
| 23. | Learning to apply course material to improve rational thinking, problem-solving, and decision making. | 3.7 | 0.0 | −.1 | −.3 | +.1 | −.1 | 0.0 | +.1 | +.3 |
| 24. | Developing specific skills, competencies, and points of view needed by professionals in the field most closely related to this course. | 3.8 | −.3 | −.2 | −.1 | +.1 | −.1 | 0.0 | 0.0 | +.3 |
| 25. | Learning how professionals in this field go about the process of gaining new knowledge. | 3.6 | −.5 | −.2 | +.1 | +.2 | −.4 | 0.0 | +.2 | +.3 |
| 26. | Developing creative capacities. | 3.5 | −.5 | −.2 | −.4 | −.1 | +.4 | −.6 | −.1 | +.2 |
| 27. | Developing a sense of personal responsibility (self-reliance, self-discipline). | 3.7 | −.3 | −.2 | −.1 | 0.0 | +.1 | −.2 | 0.0 | +.2 |
| 28. | Gaining a broader understanding and appreciation of intellectual-cultural activity (music, science, literature, etc.). | 3.1 | −.5 | −.5 | +.1 | −.2 | +.6 | −.9 | −.2 | +.1 |
| 29. | Developing skill in expressing myself orally or in writing. | 3.3 | −.9 | −.7 | −.5 | −.2 | +.9 | −.8 | −.1 | +.3 |
| 30. | Discovering the implications of the course material for understanding myself (interests, talents, values, etc.). | 3.4 | −.5 | −.4 | −.2 | +.1 | +.3 | −.4 | +.3 | +.3 |

### Teaching Methods—Stimulating the Learner

|  | | | | | | | | | | |
|---|---|---|---|---|---|---|---|---|---|---|
| 15. | Stimulated students to intellectual effort beyond that required by most courses. | 3.5 | −.1 | −.2 | +.1 | −.1 | +.1 | −.1 | 0.0 | +.2 |
| 18. | Related course material to real-life situations. | 4.1 | −.7 | −.3 | +.1 | +.3 | −.2 | 0.0 | +.3 | +.4 |
| 20. | Introduced stimulating ideas about the subject. | 3.8 | −.6 | −.4 | 0.0 | 0.0 | +.1 | −.5 | +.2 | +.3 |

## Table 9.1.  (continued)

| N | Entire Database 101710 | Math/ Statistics 5150 | Comp. & Info. Study 2777 | Biological Science 3455 | Ag. & Nat. Resources 725 | English Lang./Lit. 8013 | Accounting 2906 | Psychology 3855 | Education 8319 |
|---|---|---|---|---|---|---|---|---|---|
| *Teaching Methods—Enthusiasm* | | | | | | | | | |
| 4. Seemed enthusiastic about the subject matter. | 4.4 | -.1 | -.2 | +.1 | 0.0 | +.1 | -.2 | +.1 | +.2 |
| 7. Spoke with expressiveness and variety in tone of voice. | 4.0 | -.2 | -.3 | 0.0 | -.1 | -.2 | -.2 | +.1 | +.2 |
| 9.[a] Made presentations that were dry and dull. | 4.0 | -.1 | -.4 | -.1 | -.1 | 0.0 | -.2 | 0.0 | +.2 |
| *Teaching Methods—Communicating Content and Purpose* | | | | | | | | | |
| 10. Made it clear how each topic fit into the course. | 4.0 | -.2 | -.2 | +.1 | +.1 | 0.0 | 0.0 | +.1 | +.2 |
| 14. Summarized material in a manner that aided retention. | 3.7 | -.1 | -.3 | 0.0 | 0.0 | 0.0 | -.1 | 0.0 | +.2 |
| 16. Clearly stated the objectives of the course. | 4.1 | -.1 | -.2 | 0.0 | +.1 | +.1 | 0.0 | 0.0 | +.2 |
| 17. Explained course material clearly, and explanations were to the point. | 4.0 | -.1 | -.4 | 0.0 | 0.0 | +.1 | -.2 | 0.0 | +.1 |
| 8. Demonstrated the importance and significance of the subject matter. | 4.2 | -.2 | -.2 | +.1 | +.1 | 0.0 | 0.0 | 0.0 | +.3 |
| *Teaching Methods—Involving Students* | | | | | | | | | |
| 1. Promoted teacher-student discussion (as opposed to mere responses to questions). | 4.1 | -.3 | -.4 | -.3 | 0.0 | +.2 | -.2 | +.1 | +.3 |
| 2. Found ways to help students answer their own questions. | 3.8 | -.1 | -.3 | -.1 | 0.0 | +.2 | -.1 | 0.0 | +.2 |
| 3. Encouraged students to express themselves freely and openly. | 4.2 | -.3 | -.3 | -.2 | -.1 | +.2 | -.2 | +.1 | +.3 |
| 5. Changed approaches to meet new situations. | 3.7 | 0.0 | -.2 | 0.0 | +.1 | 0.0 | -.1 | +.1 | +.2 |

| | | Mean | | | | | | | | |
|---|---|---|---|---|---|---|---|---|---|---|
| 13. | Encouraged student comments even when they turned out to be incorrect or irrelevant. | 4.0 | -.2 | -.3 | -.2 | -.1 | -.1 | -.1 | +.1 | +.1 |
| 11. | Explained the reasons for criticisms of students' academic performance. | 3.4 | -.2 | -.2 | -.2 | 0.0 | +.3 | -.3 | -.1 | +.3 |
| | *Teaching Methods—Exams* | | | | | | | | | |
| 6.[a] | Gave examinations which stressed unnecessary memorization. | 4.0 | +.1 | -.1 | -.3 | -.2 | +.3 | -.1 | -.1 | +.1 |
| 12.[a] | Gave examination questions which were unclear. | 4.1 | 0.0 | -.3 | -.3 | -.2 | +.3 | -.2 | -.1 | +.1 |
| 19.[a] | Gave examination questions which were unreasonably detailed (picky). | 4.0 | +.1 | -.2 | -.4 | -.2 | -.3 | -.1 | -.1 | +.2 |
| | *Course Description* | | | | | | | | | |
| 31. | Amount of reading. | 3.1 | -.8 | -.1 | +.2 | -.3 | +.3 | +.3 | +.3 | 0.0 |
| 32. | Amount of work in other (nonreading) assignments. | 3.3 | +.3 | +.3 | -.2 | -.1 | 0.0 | +.4 | -.4 | +.1 |
| 33. | Difficulty of subject matter. | 3.3 | +.3 | +.1 | +.4 | -.1 | -.2 | +.5 | 0.0 | -.2 |
| 34. | Degree to which the course hung together (various topics and class activities were related to each other). | 3.8 | -.1 | -.2 | +.1 | +.1 | 0.0 | 0.0 | 0.0 | +.1 |
| | *Students' Self Ratings* | | | | | | | | | |
| 35. | I worked harder on this course than on most courses I have taken. | 3.5 | +.1 | 0.0 | +.3 | 0.0 | +.1 | +.3 | 0.0 | 0.0 |
| 36. | I had a strong desire to take this course. | 3.6 | -.4 | +.1 | 0.0 | +.3 | -.4 | +.1 | +.1 | +.1 |
| 37. | I would like to take another course from this instructor. | 3.9 | -.1 | -.3 | 0.0 | +.2 | 0.0 | -.1 | +.1 | +.1 |
| 38. | As a result of taking this course, I have more positive feelings toward this field of study. | 3.9 | -.4 | -.2 | 0.0 | +.2 | -.2 | -.3 | 0.0 | +.2 |

[a]This is a negative item where low scores are desirable. The entire database mean and difference values have been reversed so that for all items a high mean and positive differences indicate desirable ratings.

students' reports of their progress for the entire data base, we see that three objectives tie for first (items 21, 22, and 24 all have a mean of 3.8). Faculty may place somewhat higher weight on learning facts and principles, but students say they are learning professional skills and competencies at least at an equal level.

Faculty weightings of importance across these academic fields show that gaining factual knowledge (FIF 1) is first, or tied for first, in five of the eight fields. The three exceptions are English, where developing skill in oral and written expression (FIF 9) is most important; psychology, which puts discovering implications for self-understanding (FIF 10) first; and education, which weights developing professional skills and viewpoints (FIF 4) highest. Considering the focus of these last three disciplines, each of these weightings seems appropriate.

We compared the average differences for the most important course objective for the four hard with the four soft disciplines; also for the pure with the applied, and nonlife with life. None of these differed more than .3 (the approximate standard error of measurement for IDEA items). This suggests that the three Biglan dimensions do *not* lead to any systematic differences in the degree of importance faculty in different disciplines attach to the IDEA course objectives that they emphasize.

**Students' Perceptions of What Is Learned.** For students' ratings (on a 5-point scale) of how much they learned on the ten course objectives (items 21–30), the differences are either negative or zero for mathematics/statistics, computer and information science, and accounting when compared to the means on the entire data base. This indicates that at best the progress ratings in these fields tied those of the entire data base. The other fields tend to have a mix of positive, zero, and negative differences. As described above, we compared the differences of hard with soft disciplines, and so on, and found *no* systematic differences over Biglan's three dimensions.

Students' progress ratings are not random, however. We calculated Spearman *rho*'s, comparing the ranks of the importance the faculty attached to the objectives with the ranks of progress the students reported on the objectives. (Because Sixbury and Cashin [1995b] report the student means *separately* for classes where the objective was essential, important, or of minor importance, we used the corresponding table [and same database] from Cashin and Sixbury [1993] where the means *combine* essential, important, and of minor importance.) There was a strong tendency for the students to report *more learning* on the objectives the faculty weighted *more important*. That is, students report that they are learning more of what the faculty think is more important (and so, we would infer, emphasize in their teaching). However, college-level courses may still tend to emphasize memorizing facts more than developing critical thinking, problem solving, and the like. The *rho* correlations ($n = 10$), starting with the highest, were computer/information science, .97; accounting, .92; mathematics/statistics, .92; agriculture, .89; biology, .89; education, .85; psychology, .84; and English, .51 (a *rho* of .564 is significant at $p < .05$). The *rho* for the entire data base was .82. The order of the above does not result in any pattern for the Biglan clusters.

**How Students Are Taught.** On the IDEA teaching methods items (1–20), students are asked to rate (on a 5-point scale) how frequently the instructor used the method. Simply summing the differences for the teaching methods for each field yields a pattern similar to that described above with mathematics and science courses receiving the lowest ratings. The order, starting with the lowest ratings, is computer/information science, mathematics/statistics, accounting, biology, agriculture, psychology, English, and education. These differences vary considerably but are not related in any systematic way to the Biglan dimensions.

Although some fields definitely receive lower ratings than others, *when compared to the entire data base* the ratings are generally high. On a 5-point scale 3.0 is the midpoint, but the average mean for the 20 items is 3.96. To what extent these high ratings reflect student kindness versus teaching effectiveness cannot be determined from the data; probably there is a combination of the two.

Rather than listing the teaching methods items (1–20) sequentially, in Table 9.1 we grouped together items that tend to have something in common. These groupings are based in part on a factor analysis by Marsh (1994) and partly on other data from the IDEA system. Thus, items 15, 18, and 20 deal with stimulating the learners; items 4, 7, and 9, with enthusiasm; items 10, 14, 16, 17, and 8, with communicating content and purpose; items 1, 2, 3, 5, 13, and 11, with involving the students in discussion; and items 6, 12, and 19, with exams.

The items dealing with communicating content and purpose tend to be more highly correlated with the students reporting progress in gaining factual knowledge (suggesting that if you want the students to learn facts, be clear and well organized). We expected the five disciplines that emphasize gaining factual knowledge to receive higher ratings on these items (10, 14, 16, 17, and 8) than the three disciplines that did not. Such was not the case. Difference ratings on the communicating content and purpose items basically reflected the generally positive or negative ratings of the discipline rather than various items' relationship to the discipline's weighting of one objective versus another. To test this, we calculated the *rho* between the ranks of the average differences for the five communicating content and purpose items with a global item, number 37: "I would like to take another course from this instructor." The *rho* was .93. The *rho* between the same five items and the ranks for the importance of gaining factual knowledge was .46.

The above analyses were conducted *across* the eight disciplines. We wondered what the results would be if we looked *within* each of the disciplines. Specifically, we compared the average difference ratings for teaching methods that are most highly correlated with the course objective rated most important for a discipline, with the average of the differences for the teaching methods with lower correlations. For example, for FIF 1, gaining factual knowledge, the first five highest correlated teaching methods are all from communicating content and purpose: item 10 ($r$ = .69), item 8 (.68), item 17 (.64), item 14 (.63), and item 16 (.63). (These correlations were from Sixbury and Cashin, 1995a, Table 12, pages 110–112. We used the same correlation table to identify the relevant correlations for the following three course objectives.) For FIF 9—developing communication skills—which was weighted most important for English language and literature, two groups of items were relevant: involving students and stimulating the learner. For psychology's preferred objective, FIF 10—implications for self-understanding—and for education's FIF 4—professional skills and viewpoints—the pattern of correlations for the teaching methods was more mixed. For psychology, the involving-students items fit best. For education, the communicating content and purpose items tended to have the higher correlations.

Having identified the relevant teaching methods, we compared the average difference on those items with the average difference on the remaining items. For example, for the five disciplines where FIF 1 was weighted highest, we averaged the differences for these five items and compared that average with the average difference of the remaining fifteen teaching methods. For all five disciplines, on average the students rated the faculty as using the communicating content and purpose items more frequently than the other fifteen items. For FIF 9—developing communication skills—the average differences of these nine teaching methods was higher than the average for the remaining eleven items. For FIF 10—implications for self-understanding—the average difference for the six involving-students items was higher than those for the rest of the items. Contrary to our expectations, however, the average difference for items relevant to FIF 4—professional skills and viewpoints—was *lower* than the average difference for the other items (.22 compared to .20). Nevertheless, for seven of the eight disciplines, the instructors received higher ratings on the teaching methods *most relevant* to the most important course objective for the discipline. These results *just* reach statistical significance using the sign test ($p$ = .035).

## Conclusion

Several conclusions can be reached from these findings. First, academic disciplines differ in the course objectives they emphasize (as Franklin and Theall, 1992, also found), but the emphases do not seem to be systematically related to the Biglan clusters. Second, despite the rhetoric of the past several years recommending the teaching of higher-order skills like critical thinking and problem solving, many disciplines still appear to be focusing more on teaching facts (again, as Franklin and Theall found). Whether being taught facts or something higher, however, students report that they make progress in learning whatever the specific discipline emphasizes. Finally, some data support the hypothesis that one of the reasons different disciplines receive different ratings is that they have different course objectives for which *different teaching methods are appropriate*. Logically, it follows that students will give higher ratings on teaching methods that are more appropriate for learning those objectives. Thus, we are becoming clearer about the differences that exist in student ratings of various fields, but based on the eight fields studied here Biglan's clusters are not the explanation.

## References

Barnes, L.L.B., and Barnes, M. W. "Academic Discipline and Generalizability of Student Evaluations of Instruction." *Research in Higher Education,* 1993, *34,* 135–149.

Biglan, A. "The Characteristics of Subject Matter in Different Academic Areas." *Journal of Applied Psychology,* 1973a, 57 (3), 195–203.

Biglan, A. "Relationships Between Subject Matter Characteristics and the Structure and Output of University Departments." *Journal of Applied Psychology,* 1973b, 57 (3), 204–213.

Bloom, B. S., Engelhart, M. D., Furst, E. J., Hill, W. H., and Krathwohl, D. R. *Taxonomy of Educational Objectives: Handbook I, the Cognitive Domain.* New York: David McKay, 1956.

Cashin, W. E. "Students Do Rate Different Academic Fields Differently." In M. Theall and J. Franklin (eds.), *Student Ratings of Instruction: Issues for Improving Practice.* New Directions for Teaching and Learning, no. 43. San Francisco: Jossey-Bass, 1990.

Cashin, W. E., and Clegg, V. L. *Are Student Ratings of Different Academic Fields Different?* Paper presented at the annual meeting of the American Educational Research Association, Chicago, April 1987. (ED 286 935)

Cashin, W. E., Noma, A., and Hanna, G. S. *IDEA Technical Report No. 6: Comparative Data by Academic Field.* Manhattan: Kansas State University, Center for Faculty Evaluation and Development, 1987.

Cashin, W. E., and Sixbury, G. R., *IDEA Technical Report No. 8: Comparative Data by Academic Field.* Manhattan: Kansas State University, Center for Faculty Evaluation and Development, 1993.

Cohen, P. A. "Student Ratings of Instruction and Student Achievement: A Meta-Analysis of Multisection Validity Studies." *Review of Educational Research,* 1981, *51,* 281–309.

Educational Testing Service. *Student Instructional Report: Comparative Data Guide for Four-Year Colleges and Universities.* Princeton, N.J.: Educational Testing Service, 1982a.

Educational Testing Service. *Student Instructional Report: Comparative Data Guide for Two-Year Colleges and Technical Institutions.* Princeton, N.J.: Educational Testing Service, 1982b.

Feldman, K. A. "Course Characteristics and College Students' Ratings of Their Teachers: What We Know and What We Don't." *Research in Higher Education,* 1978, *9,* 199–242.

Feldman, K. A. "The Association Between Student Ratings of Specific Instructional Dimensions and Student Achievement: Refining and Extending the Synthesis of Data from Multisection Validity Studies." *Research in Higher Education,* 1989, *30,* 583–645.

Franklin, J., and Theall, M. *Disciplinary Differences: Instructional Goals and Activities, Measures of Student Performance, and Student Ratings of Instruction.* Paper presented at the annual meeting of the American Educational Research Association, San Francisco, April 1992. (ED 346 786)

Marsh, H. W. "Weighting for the Right Criteria in the IDEA System: Global and Specific Ratings of Teaching Effectiveness and Their Relation to Course Objectives." *Journal of Educational Psychology,* 1994, *86,* 631–648.

Neumann, Y., and Neumann, L. "Characteristics of Academic Areas and Students' Evaluation of Instruction." *Research in Higher Education,* 1983, *19,* 323–334.

Sixbury, G. R., and Cashin, W. E. *IDEA Technical Report No. 9: Description of Database for the IDEA Diagnostic Form.* Manhattan: Kansas State University, Center for Faculty Evaluation and Development, 1995a.

Sixbury, G. R., and Cashin, W. E. *IDEA Technical Report No. 10: Comparative Data by Academic Field.* Manhattan: Kansas State University, Center for Faculty Evaluation and Development, 1995b.

Smith, R. A., and Cranton, P. A. "Students' Perceptions of Teaching Skills and Overall Effectiveness Across Instructional Settings." *Research in Higher Education,* 1992, *33,* 747–764.

*William E. Cashin is director of the Center for Faculty Evaluation and Development at Kansas State University.*

*Ronald G. Downey is director of institutional research and analysis at Kansas State University.*

*Students in different disciplines develop characteristic ways of learning
based on their perceptions of what is required in their academic work.
Within a discipline, effective learning involves interplay between the
characteristics of the student and those of the learning environment
that is provided by the teacher and the department.*

# Approaches to Studying and Perceptions of the Learning Environment Across Disciplines

*Noel Entwistle, Hilary Tait*

In Britain, research into higher education has sought to describe differences in
study methods and their links with subsequent academic success across contrasting disciplines. In the 1960s, attempts were made to predict levels of academic performance in terms of relatively stable and general traits of students,
such as ability and personality (Entwistle and Wilson, 1977). These studies
indicated disciplinary differences in the correlates of academic success, but
their contribution to improving teaching and learning was disappointing. As
a result, subsequent research focused directly on constructs which describe the
ways in which students learn and study, and these differences have been shown
to depend on the particular learning environment provided by faculty members and by the institution as a whole.

## Styles of Learning and Approaches to Studying

The main problem with the early studies was their reliance on the measurement
of "traits" derived from the psychological literature, and their dependency on surveys and correlational analysis. These techniques tended to obscure important
variations among individual students and also to pay insufficient attention to the
processes of studying. In the mid 1970s, a series of studies looked at studying in
contexts similar to those experienced by students in their everyday academic
work; these studies made much greater use of qualitative research methods.

**Approaches to Learning.** Marton and his colleagues in Gothenburg
published an influential series of articles describing how students went about

reading an academic article (Marton and Saljo, 1976, 1984). They concluded that the most important difference among students was in their intention. Students who intended to understand the author's meaning adopted what came to be called a *deep approach*, while those who were more concerned to reproduce isolated pieces of information on which they expected to be tested used a *surface approach*. Subsequent research has shown that the deep approach is associated with intrinsic motivation, or interest in the subject itself, while the surface approach is driven by either fear of failure or instrumental motivation (Biggs, 1987; Entwistle, 1988). The main defining features of these approaches are shown in Table 10.1.

**Learning Styles and Strategies.** At about the same time, distinctive styles and strategies were being identified in naturalistic experiments by Pask (1976). He found that students seeking to understand academic material used distinctively different strategies to do so, and he came to the conclusion that students had differing *styles of learning*. Some students used a *serialist* strategy involving operation learning in which they learned the material step-by-step, concentrating initially on the details and logical connections within the material presented, and looking for analogies or interconnections with other ideas only toward the end of the learning process. Other students preferred a *holist* strategy in which they built up an overall picture to guide their learning, looked for analogies and related ideas through a process of comprehension learning, and began examining the detail and logical connections only much later on in their attempts to achieve full understanding.

Each style can exist in extreme forms, which lead to *learning pathologies* and incomplete understanding. Extreme holists tend to make invalid analogies and reach conclusions prematurely or make generalizations on incomplete evidence, a pathology that Pask calls "globe-trotting." Persistent serialists, in contrast, make insufficient use of analogies; in the extreme, their "improvidence" in learning reduces itself to an overreliance on procedural, fact-based learning, equivalent to a surface approach. Pask found that students with a strong preferred style learn ineffectively and slowly when faced with material organized according to opposite principles (Pask, 1988). However, some students seem at home with either style: they are *versatile* in their ability to use either operation or comprehension processes with equal ease.

In considering the defining features of the deep approach in Table 10.1, it can be seen that there are distinctive learning processes associated with it. Students seeking understanding use two quite different learning processes: one involves relating ideas and looking for patterns and principles, and the other depends on checking evidence and examining the logic of the argument presented. These processes are similar to comprehension learning and operation learning (Entwistle, in press). Disciplinary differences in styles are considered alongside differences in study orientations in the subsection that follows.

**Approaches to Studying.** A longitudinal study conducted at Lancaster (Entwistle and Ramsden, 1983) used both interviews and questionnaires to collect data. The interviews in this study and in several others (for example,

## Table 10.1. Defining Features of Approaches to Learning

| Approach | Characterization of Approach | Intention | Defining Features |
|---|---|---|---|
| Deep | Transforming | To understand material for oneself | Being actively interested in the course content |
| | | | Relating ideas to previous knowledge and experience |
| | | | Looking for patterns and underlying principles |
| | | | Checking evidence and relating it to conclusions |
| | | | Examining logic and argument cautiously and critically |
| Surface | Reproducing | To cope with content and tasks set | Studying without reflecting on either purpose or strategy |
| | | | Treating the course as unrelated bits of knowledge |
| | | | Finding difficulty in making sense of new ideas presented |
| | | | Memorizing facts and procedures routinely |
| | | | Feeling undue pressure and worry about work |
| Strategic | Organizing | To excel on assessed work | Being alert to assessment requirements and criteria |
| | | | Gearing work to the perceived preferences of lecturers |
| | | | Putting consistent effort into studying |
| | | | Finding the right conditions and materials for studying |
| | | | Managing time and effort effectively to maximize grades |

Marton, Hounsell, and Entwistle, 1996) confirmed the importance of the distinction between deep and surface approaches but indicated that in everyday studying (as opposed to the naturalistic experiment), where assessment was crucial to the student, another approach—the *strategic*—was identified. It depended on an intention to excel in assessment terms and was associated with the competitive form of motivation often called "need for achievement." The defining features of this approach are also found in Table 10.1.

The questionnaire data were obtained from 2,208 students in a national sample which covered six honors disciplines. These data were collected using the *Approaches to Studying Inventory* (Entwistle and Ramsden, 1983). The four main dimensions scored from the inventory responses were called meaning orientation (representing an extended definition of the deep approach), reproducing orientation (surface approach and improvidence), achieving orientation (strategic approach), and nonacademic orientation (disorganized study methods, negative attitudes, and globe-trotting). The mean scores, and correlations with a rating of academic progress in the penultimate year of study, are shown in Table 10.2, presented for the six disciplines involved.

Certain patterns in the mean scores can be discerned, although the differences are generally small. Tests of statistical significance among departments were not carried out. Students specializing in English have higher scores on meaning orientation and holistic styles of learning, and lower scores on both achieving and nonacademic orientations. History students have rather average scores, although like the English students they tend to have quite low scores on both achieving and nonacademic orientations. Psychology students share with the English students higher scores on the meaning orientation but also have equally high scores on the nonacademic orientation. This apparent contradiction probably reflects the existence of two groups of students taking psychology, one as a vocational commitment and one as a "make weight." Economics students show high scores on reproducing and achieving orientations and serialist style, combined with low scores on meaning orientation and holistic style. In physics, the students are distinguished only by having a higher achieving orientation, a characteristic they share with the engineers, who also score high on serialist style but low in both meaning and reproducing orientations. The general conclusions in this analysis were that students studying science or economics do differ from the other students in their learning style and that the emphasis on serialist strategies may well be a necessary characteristic in these subject areas.

To look at the correlations with ratings of academic progress, the patterns across the six disciplines seem quite similar, although there are differences in the relative strengths of the relationships. For example, meaning orientation is less of an advantage in physics and engineering (implying that these are emphasized less in assessment procedures), while a reproducing orientation is less of a disadvantage in psychology but, together with a serialist style, is more heavily penalized in the marking of both history and English. Being strategic is less important in the two art-based subjects, while history students who have

## Table 10.2. Mean Scores and Correlations with Academic Progress by Honors Discipline

| Scale (Sample size) | English (282) | | History (209) | | Economics (450) | | Psychology (402) | | Physics (357) | | Engineering (508) | |
|---|---|---|---|---|---|---|---|---|---|---|---|---|
| | Mean | r | M | r | M | r | M | r | M | r | M | r |
| Orientation | | | | | | | | | | | | |
| Meaning | 40.6 | 0.23 | 39.4 | 0.27 | 36.7 | 0.24 | 40.6 | 0.20 | 38.0 | 0.17 | 37.2 | 0.14 |
| Reproducing | 32.5 | −0.39 | 32.8 | −0.35 | 37.0 | −0.24 | 33.8 | −0.14 | 34.7 | −0.26 | 31.0 | −0.23 |
| Achieving | 18.8 | 0.27 | 18.8 | 0.24 | 20.3 | 0.38 | 19.0 | 0.38 | 20.4 | 0.40 | 21.2 | 0.28 |
| Nonacademic | 21.5 | −0.36 | 21.3 | −0.27 | 22.8 | −0.39 | 23.4 | −0.37 | 22.8 | −0.44 | 22.7 | −0.40 |
| Style | | | | | | | | | | | | |
| Holistic | 11.0 | −0.02 | 8.7 | 0.01 | 7.7 | −0.02 | 9.0 | 0.00 | 8.2 | −0.08 | 8.0 | −0.06 |
| Serialist | 8.6 | −0.23 | 9.8 | −0.23 | 10.8 | −0.06 | 9.2 | −0.02 | 10.1 | −0.06 | 11.1 | −0.09 |

a nonacademic orientation do less badly than students with a nonacademic orientation do in most other subjects.

**Forms of Understanding.** In very recent research, the ways in which understanding is sought during review for final examinations (revision, in British parlance) has been investigated using exploratory in-depth interviews of students taking psychology, zoology, medicine, and, subsequently, social history (Entwistle and Entwistle, 1991; Entwistle, 1995). Students were found to differ in the *forms of understanding* which they sought. These differences can be described in terms of variations in the breadth, depth, and structure of their understandings. Some students relied heavily on their lecture notes alone and showed a form of understanding which was narrow and shallow and which reproduced the structure provided by the lecturer. Other students had read more widely and developed their own structure to make sense of the topic being reviewed. Within this latter group there were differences in the extent to which the students were either directing the form of their understanding toward the specific requirements of the examination or more concerned with the completeness of their own understandings. The former group tended to be more successful in the examinations, while the latter group seemed to develop forms of understanding which showed the best overall grasp of the nature of the discipline.

In reviewing, most students followed similar procedures, but to a different extent and with a different balance. They read through their complete set of notes and then made condensed review notes, often reducing those further to a single page of outline notes for each topic. These outline notes were then used to check their understanding. Once the outline was understood, students sought to learn by rote the details needed to justify the explanations they expected to give in the examinations. When asked how they remembered the material they had revised, many of the students described an experience of "seeing" the relevant page of their review notes, not to the point of being able to read off the words, but knowing the structure and shape of the main points and argument, which, they found, pulled in the details they had rote learned as they were required. This quasi-sensory experience of well-structured understandings created through intensive intellectual effort led to the introduction of the term *knowledge objects* (Entwistle and Marton, 1994), which seemed to help students develop logically structured answers in exams in response to the questions asked. To a lesser extent, knowledge objects were developed during the researching and organizing of course work essays (term papers), but apparently only where the student had engaged personally with the topic (Entwistle, 1995).

So far, these studies have been based on small samples and thus it is difficult to make comments about interdisciplinary differences. However, it is clear that the medical students in the sample relied much more heavily on rote learning than the other students, at least in preparing for preclinical exams. There was also a suggestion that the zoologists were relying more on visualization; but since women were overrepresented in this group, this may reflect a gender, rather than a disciplinary, difference. The exploration of disciplinary differences in the forms of understanding seems to be an area well worth exploring further.

## Approaches to Studying and Perceptions of Learning Environments

In the analyses reported above, students taking the same discipline from many different departments were analyzed together, ignoring the possible effects of different experiences of teaching on their approaches to studying. But a wide range of research on student learning (see, for example, the studies reported in Entwistle, 1991) has indicated ways in which teaching and assessment influence how students learn in different departments.

**Influences on the Approach to Learning.** Assessments that emphasize the correct reproduction of facts (as do most multiple-choice and short-answer tests) and overly demanding syllabuses both shift students toward a surface approach, whereas assessment and teaching that demand understanding—with time to assimilate the material—encourage a deep approach. This finding applies equally to science and arts departments, but the greater use of objective testing in the sciences and social sciences, and the packed syllabuses in the sciences, lead to a greater prevalence of surface approaches in those areas. Such differences are not a necessary characteristic of the discipline, and in the departments included in the Lancaster survey there were substantial differences among all six disciplines in the range of scores on approaches to learning (Entwistle and Ramsden, 1983, pp. 241–243).

**Contrasting Perceptions of the Learning Environment.** The term *learning environment* has been used to describe the whole set of learning opportunities which are provided within a course: lectures, small group discussions, individual tutorials, set reading, assignments, tests, and the increasing variety of learning resources becoming available through technology-based learning. As indicated, aspects of the learning environment are already known to affect the approaches to learning which students adopt and so also the quality of the learning outcomes. While students necessarily experience the same learning environment, they perceive it in different ways. And the direct influence on the approach to learning comes from the subjective *perception,* rather than from the objectively described environment.

A clear demonstration of this effect comes from the work of the Gothenburg group. Fransson (1977) designed a learning experiment in which students learned the same material under different conditions. Some students read an article which referred to proposed changes in assessment procedures in their own department, while other students from a different department read the same article. The expected relevance of, and interest in, the content was thus expected to be different for the two groups. Within each of these groups, the level of stress under which the learning took place was also varied. Half of the students read the article under relaxed conditions, while the other half were put under stress by indicating that members of the group would have to explain the text afterwards to the group as a whole. Both groups were tested in the same way, by answering written questions and completing a short questionnaire about their perceptions of the experiment. No significant differences were found between the experimental groups, but when the data were reanalyzed in terms of those who had *felt* the article to be interesting, and those who had *felt* anxious in the stressful situation, there were significant differences. Students who had found the article interesting were more likely to have sought understanding (deep approach), while those who had felt anxious had concentrated on question-spotting (surface approach).

Recently, Meyer (1991) has introduced the idea of *study orchestration,* which suggests a relationship between students' approaches to studying and their perceptions of the learning environment. For example, students showing a deep approach are usually able to perceive those aspects of the learning environment which can support a deep approach and then use those supports appropriately. However, some students show an unusual mismatch between their intention to seek understanding and their perceptions of the learning environment (Meyer, Parsons, and Dunne, 1990; Entwistle, Meyer, and Tait, 1991). Such "disintegrated" patterns of study strategies and perceptions seem to lead to specific difficulties for students. In particular, some students have the intention to understand but seem to find it almost impossible to make use of the opportunities provided in the learning environment to develop their understanding effectively (Calder, 1989).

Students also *prefer* learning environments that enable them to study in the ways they have developed as a habit. From Pask's (1988) work, it seems that students will prefer a teaching style which directly supports their own learning style. Similarly, Entwistle and Tait (1990) found that students who reported themselves as adopting surface approaches to learning preferred teaching and assessment procedures which supported that approach, whereas students reporting deep approaches preferred courses which were intellectually challenging and assessment methods which allowed them to demonstrate their understanding. A direct consequence of this effect is that the ratings which students make of their lecturers will depend on the extent to which the lecturer's style fits what individual students prefer. Thus, a lecturer seeking to encourage reflection and insisting on understanding may be rated highly by colleagues but is likely to get rather poor ratings from students who want no more than an easy ride toward reproductive answers in assessment (Entwistle and Tait, 1994).

## Implications for Teaching and Learning in Higher Education

The research on student learning reported above has indicated some differences between disciplines, but the main thrust of this research has in fact been toward establishing *general* principles to guide effective teaching and learning

(Entwistle, Thompson, and Tait, 1992). Looking at teaching and learning through comparisons, particularly between engineering and psychology (Tait, 1992), has led to the identification of a series of aspects which do affect the quality of learning generally but also are of differential importance in different areas of study.

For example, in an anatomy department, Eizenberg (1988) described the measures taken to support a deep approach to studying. The department had recognized that their teaching and assessment procedures carried a strong implication for students that accurate recall of facts was of most consequence. In reality, academic staff were more concerned with the understanding of principles, supported by knowledge of facts. By systematic analysis of the learning environment, they were able to change students' perceptions of what was required of them and so influence their approaches to studying. It seems that the single most influential feature of the learning environment is the nature of the assessment procedures, and Thomas and Bain (1984) showed clearly how a change from multiple-choice to essay-type examinations had shifted the overall tendency of the students from surface approach toward deep approach. However, Eizenberg (1988) stressed that any component within the learning environment which contradicted the direction of influence of the other components might prevent the intended effect from being achieved. Thus, a clear implication for effective teaching is that all aspects of a course must convey the same message to students regarding what will be rewarded through assignments and examinations.

Each discipline will be expecting rather a different balance of knowledge and skills to be developed, but the starting point for each department should be an analysis of their current learning environment to discover whether the desired approaches to learning are being supported. The general principles derived from the research on student learning will then allow departments to decide for themselves how they should modify their teaching arrangements to provide an environment which will support high-quality student learning (Biggs, 1989). Teaching staff should be encouraged to look carefully at the learning environment of their students and to confirm that what is being offered matches what the department is trying to achieve.

In any such review of their teaching, departments also should look carefully at the provision they make for systematic training in effective study methods and skills. Unfortunately, traditional study skills workshops have proved rather ineffective (Gibbs, 1981). Training needs to be introduced when students recognize the need for refining particular skills, and wherever possible the training should be offered as part of the normal teaching of a course. But the type of training is still important. Above all, it should encourage the students to reflect on their own ways of studying and consider which skills and strategies they need to improve (Biggs, 1987). The habit of monitoring the effectiveness of their studying brings continuing benefit to students.

Students need to acquire more than just discipline-specific *knowledge* when studying a course in higher education; they also need to develop relevant study skills. There is, however, a serious problem in teaching study skills within courses. Academic staff feel unprepared for this type of teaching and want to have it carried out by experts. One alternative is for departments to provide access to pre-prepared, discipline-specific study skills support within their own courses. This strategy has been used at Edinburgh by developing a computer-based advice system in Hypertext which identifies the apparent weaknesses reported by individual students and offers advice on those areas (Tait and Entwistle, in press). This advice has been derived, as far as possible, from research findings and uses extracts from interviews with students to illustrate the study strategies which other students in similar disciplines have found helpful. The software package has been directed toward departments and offers opportunities for incorporating advice specific to that discipline or department. The supporting documentation also encourages teaching staff to take account of common weaknesses in studying. It does so not just by providing training in study skills but also by examining the learning environment that staff are providing for students (lest they be partly responsible for common weaknesses in students' study approaches). Such software can play a key role in helping departments to provide environments that will encourage high-quality student learning.

## References

Biggs, J. B. *Student Approaches to Learning and Studying.* Melbourne: Australian Council for Educational Research, 1987.

Biggs, J. B. "Approaches to Enhancement of Tertiary Teaching." *Higher Education Research and Development,* 1989, *8,* 7–25.

Calder, I. "The Study and Learning Strategies of Students in a New Zealand Tertiary Institution." Unpublished Ph.D. thesis, University of Waikato, New Zealand, 1989.

Eizenberg, N. "Approaches to Learning Anatomy: Developing a Programme for Preclinical Medical Students." In P. Ramsden (ed.), *Improving Learning: New Perspectives.* London: Kogan Page, 1988.

Entwistle, N. J. "Motivational Factors in Students' Approaches to Learning." In R. R. Schmeck (ed.), *Learning Strategies and Learning Styles.* New York: Plenum Press, 1988.

Entwistle, N. J. (ed.). "Approaches to Learning and Perceptions of the Learning Environment." *Higher Education,* 1991, *22* (3).

Entwistle, N. J. "Frameworks for Understanding, as Experienced in Essay Writing and in Preparing for Examinations." *Educational Psychologist,* 1995, *30,* 47–54.

Entwistle, N. J. "The Nature of Academic Understanding." In T. Helstrup, G. Kaufmann, and K. H. Teigen (eds.), *Problem Solving and Cognitive Processes: Essays in Honor of Kjell Raaheim.* Bergen, Germany: Universitetsforlaget, in press.

Entwistle, N. J., and Entwistle, A. C. "Contrasting Forms of Understanding for Degree Examinations: The Student Experience and Its Implications." *Higher Education,* 1991, *22,* 205–227.

Entwistle, N. J., and Marton, F. "Knowledge Objects: Understandings Constituted Through Intensive Academic Study." *British Journal of Educational Psychology,* 1994, *64,* 161–178.

Entwistle, N. J., Meyer, J.H.F., and Tait, H. "Student Failure: Disintegrated Patterns of Study Strategies and Perceptions of the Learning Environment." *Higher Education,* 1991, *22,* 249–261.

Entwistle, N. J., and Ramsden, P. *Understanding Student Learning.* London: Croom Helm, 1983.

Entwistle, N. J., and Tait, H. "Approaches to Learning, Evaluations of Teaching, and Preferences for Contrasting Academic Environments." *Higher Education,* 1990, *19,* 169–194.

Entwistle, N. J., and Tait, H. "Approaches to Studying and Preferences for Teaching in Higher Education: Implications for Student Ratings." *Instructional Evaluation and Faculty Development,* 1994, *14,* 2–10.

Entwistle, N. J., Thompson, S., and Tait, H. *Guidelines for Promoting Effective Learning in Higher Education.* Edinburgh: Centre for Research on Learning and Instruction, University of Edinburgh, 1992.

Entwistle, N. J., and Wilson, J. D. *Degrees of Excellence: The Academic Achievement Game.* London: Hodder & Stoughton, 1977.

Fransson, A. "On Qualitative Differences in Learning. IV: Effects of Intrinsic Motivation and Extrinsic Test Anxiety on Process and Outcome." *British Journal of Educational Psychology,* 1977, *47,* 244–257.

Gibbs, G. *Teaching Students to Learn: a Student-Centred Approach.* Milton Keynes, England: Open University Press, 1981.

Marton, F., Hounsell, D. J., and Entwistle, N. J. *The Experience of Learning.* Edinburgh: Scottish Academic Press, 1996.

Marton, F., and Saljo, R. "On Qualitative Differences in Learning. I: Outcome and Process." *British Journal of Educational Psychology,* 1976, *46,* 4–11.

Marton, F., and Saljo, R. "Approaches to Learning." In F. Marton, D. J. Hounsell, and N. J. Entwistle (eds.), *The Experience of Learning.* Edinburgh: Scottish Academic Press, 1984.

Meyer, J.H.F. "Study Orchestration: The Manifestation, Interpretation, and Consequences of Contextualised Approaches to Studying." *Higher Education,* 1991, *22,* 297–316.

Meyer J.H.F., Parsons, P., and Dunne, T. T. "Individual Study Orchestrations and Their Association with Learning Outcome." *Higher Education,* 1990, *20,* 67–89.

Pask, G. "Styles and Strategies of Learning." *British Journal of Educational Psychology,* 1976, *46,* 128–148.

Pask, G. "Learning Strategies, Teaching Strategies and Conceptual or Learning Style." In R. R. Schmeck (ed.), *Learning Strategies and Learning Styles.* New York: Plenum Press, 1988.

Tait, H. "Students' Perceptions of Teaching in Relation to Their Approaches to Studying." Unpublished Ph.D. thesis, Department of Education, University of Edinburgh, 1992.

Tait, H., and Entwistle, N. J. "Identifying Students at Risk Through Ineffective Study Strategies." *Higher Education,* in press.

Thomas, P. R., and Bain, J. D. "Contextual Dependence of Learning Approaches: The Effects of Assessments." *Human Learning,* 1984, *3,* 227–240.

*Noel Entwistle is Bell Professor of Education at the University of Edinburgh and director of the Centre for Research on Learning and Instruction (CRLI). He is also coordinating editor of the journal* Higher Education.

*Hilary Tait is a research associate at the Centre for Research on Learning and Instruction (CRLI) and editorial assistant for the journal* Higher Education.

*College students bring a variety of perceptions to the classroom about what it takes to succeed in a discipline. This chapter focuses on ways to modify potentially maladaptive perceptions into more adaptive ones, by focusing on a therapeutic technique referred to as attributional retraining.*

# Disciplinary Differences in Students' Perceptions of Success: Modifying Misperceptions with Attributional Retraining

*Verena H. Menec, Raymond P. Perry*

What does it take to succeed in a particular discipline? Stereotypes suggest that innate ability or talent are important in such fields as mathematics, fine arts, and music. A student's studying efforts or study strategies are more likely to be perceived as determinants of success in psychology or history. These perceptions about success are often implicit, perpetuated by classmates, teachers, or even the popular media. They are reflected in statements on the order of "You either get math or you don't," and in the common perception that great figures in a field, such as Einstein or Picasso, came by their obvious skills exclusively through innate ability rather than by putting effort into their work. As these stereotypes are internalized by students, they affect their perceptions of performance, self-esteem, and choice of whether to continue in a given discipline. A student who performs poorly on a mathematics test, for example, may come to the conclusion "I can't do math," which in turn may lead to the decision to drop the course or not take further mathematics courses.

In the present chapter, we describe a therapeutic technique that is designed to modify students' (mis)perceptions of their successes and failures. This technique is referred to as *attributional retraining*; it is based on attributional theories of motivation (Abramson, Seligman, and Teasdale, 1978; Weiner, 1986). The theoretical underpinnings of attributional retraining are described here, focusing specifically on Weiner's theory, followed by a discussion of the research evidence regarding the effectiveness of attributional retraining. Lastly, we address the implications of this literature for college teaching.

## Causal Attributions and Their Consequences

Weiner (1986) proposes that people routinely and spontaneously search for the causes of events in their lives. The explanations or attributions they make then impact on emotions and expectations, with emotions and expectations jointly contributing to motivated behavior. Although comments like "I had a bad day," "I should have studied more," and "I'm not good at this" would appear to be quite different, Weiner argues that they can all be described in terms of three underlying dimensions: locus of causality (internal, external), stability (stable, unstable), and controllability (controllable, uncontrollable). These dimensions are critical because they determine specific emotions as well as expectations of future success.

Consider the student who fails a test and attributes this failure to lack of ability. Because ability is typically perceived as internal, stable, and uncontrollable, the student's self-esteem will suffer, expectations of success in the future will decrease, and feelings of shame will be invoked. In effect, the student expects failure to reoccur no matter what she or he does. Not surprisingly, the student is therefore unlikely to engage in any productive studying efforts, class attendance may decrease, or the student may pay less attention in class. This lack of motivation, in turn, almost guarantees poor performance on subsequent tests and may eventually cause the individual to give up entirely and drop out of the course.

Contrast this negative motivational profile with one in which a student attributes failure to lack of effort or inadequate study strategies, both of which are internal, unstable, and controllable attributions. In this case, expectations of success in the future are maintained and high expectations of success, combined with feelings of guilt, will provide the impetus for the student to work extra hard to succeed on the next test. Trying harder, although it certainly does not guarantee success, at least increases the chances to do well on future tests.

An important question is why one student would attribute his or her performance to lack of ability, whereas other students explain their failures in terms of more adaptive attributions such as lack of effort or ineffective study strategies. Research shows that maladaptive attributional profiles, associated with lack of motivation and helplessness, are evident as early as elementary school (see, for example, Diener and Dweck, 1978). Characteristics that children bring to the classroom, such as their self-esteem, gender, cultural background, and so on all contribute to the development of such attributional profiles. We propose in this chapter that a further factor that shapes students' attributions is the existence of stereotypes, or myths, associated with academic disciplines.

These myths are transmitted by siblings, teachers, the popular media, and even talking Barbie dolls who make comments like "Math is tough!" Such internalized beliefs affect children's attributions for their performances across disciplines from the first grade on. As a result, a girl who already has the mindset that math is not something for girls will explain her successes and failures very differently than the boy who considers it a "masculine" field. Poor performance in a math course may therefore be readily interpreted as evidence for lack of math ability by the girl but ascribed to lack of preparation by the boy.

Disciplinary differences in attributions that are established and reinforced over the early school years and in high school should also be evident in college. In our own research with college students, we found evidence for such differences in attributions across disciplines. Preliminary analyses of these data indicate that in a biology course, science students—when compared to students enrolled in the faculty of arts—attributed their performance more to ability, interest, and luck, but less to course difficulty. This attributional profile can be considered adaptive as it reflects an internal locus, that is, a willingness to take responsibility for one's performance. The pattern of findings was quite different in a psychology course, however. Most notably, for ability attributions no differences emerged between science and arts students. In fact, science and arts students differed on only one attribution, with science students attributing their performance in the psychology course less to their interest than did arts students. Thus, science students stressed ability as a contributor to their performance only in a science, but not in a social science course. This disciplinary difference in attributions makes sense given the common assumption that innate ability contributes more to success in science courses than to success in a social science course such as psychology. While our data on disciplinary differences in attributions is preliminary, the topic of such differences certainly warrants further examination.

In general terms, then, certain students can be at risk in a particular discipline if they believe that they lack the ability to succeed. In this respect, researchers have long been interested in the question of why there are not more women or minority groups in mathematics and engineering (Fox, Brody, and Tobin, 1980). While this raises the question of what factors socialize women and minority groups away from the "hard" sciences, the critical issue from our perspective is that students' perceptions shape how they strive to achieve and their career choices, and that these perceptions can be changed. Attributional retraining is one technique designed to do precisely that.

## Attributional Retraining

Although attributional retraining is a technique that has been investigated extensively with children, it has received relatively less attention in higher education. Available studies are consistent and clearly indicate that attributional retraining is an effective method for assisting students, particularly those at risk. For a detailed discussion of this research, we refer the interested reader to a literature review by Perry, Hechter, Menec, and Weinberg (1993).

Consider the seminal study by Wilson and Linville (1982). These researchers selected first-year college students who seemed to be at risk according to several criteria, the most important being that they were worried about their grade point average (GPA) and thought they should have done better in their courses. These students were then assigned to either an attributional retraining group or a control group. Students in the attributional retraining condition were first given a summary of an actual survey which showed that, although many students have difficulties in their first year at university, GPAs improve significantly from the first year to upperclass years. After this, the students watched a videotape of senior students who provided testimonials that their GPA had improved over time. Lastly, a videotape was shown of a psychology professor who discussed the results of the survey. The purpose of all of this information was to change stable attributions (the perception that GPA is determined by factors that cannot be modified, as in the case of aptitude) to more unstable ones (first-year students tend to do poorly because of the novel environment and requirements, homesickness, lack of effective study strategies, etc.).

Among other measures, Wilson and Linville examined students' performance on a reading comprehension task and an anagram task, both administered one week after the intervention. The researchers also kept track of students' GPAs at the end of the first year and sophomore year. The results of the study showed that students who received attributional retraining performed better on the reading comprehension task administered immediately after the attributional retraining intervention. They also obtained higher GPAs one year following the study than those in the control group.

Even though Wilson and Linville's findings were questioned by other researchers on methodological and statistical grounds, subsequent studies confirmed their conclusion that attributional retraining improves students' achievement both in the short-term and long-term (for example, Perry and Penner, 1990; Van Overwalle and De Metsenaere, 1990).

**Attributional Retraining Methods.** Since Wilson and Linville's study, researchers have focused primarily on changing uncontrollable, stable attributions (as with lack of ability) to controllable, unstable ones (such as lack of effort or poor study strategies) (see, for example, Menec and others, 1994; Perry and Penner, 1990; Van Overwalle and De Metsenaere, 1990). In effect, the message conveyed is this: Try harder and work smarter. Attributional retraining is usually provided by means of a videotape, which shows senior students discussing their academic performance and the reasons for their successes or failures.

For example, in a videotape that we have successfully used in our research, two students discuss their first year at university. One student relates that he performed quite poorly on several tests and started to doubt his abilities. He then realized, however, that he really had not studied very much; upon acknowledging this he started to put much more effort into the course, with the consequence that his performance improved dramatically. A second student then describes a similar scenario of having failed but focuses on the importance of good study strategies and describes how changing her strategies enhanced her performance. Finally, a psychology professor summarizes the most important points of the message.

While the videotape is common to most attributional retraining studies, some researchers have supplemented it with a discussion session (for example, Perry, Struthers, Menec, and Weinberg, 1994; Van Overwalle and De Metsenaere, 1990). This discussion allows participants to talk about their own experiences and perceptions of successes and failures. What is noteworthy is that attributional retraining interventions are quite short, ranging from eight minutes to one hour. The finding that they are able to increase motivation and achievement, both in the short-term and long-term, is therefore especially significant.

How different retraining techniques compare has received little attention to date. For example, is a discussion about maladaptive attributions better than simply viewing a videotape, a procedure that requires no active involvement from students? Our research (Perry, Struthers, Menec, and Weinberg, 1994) indicates that a videotape combined with a discussion is more effective in the long term than a videotape only. In fact, attributional retraining transmitted via a videotape and a discussion enhanced students' performance on an actual course test by 6 percent. In practical terms, this reflects an increase of about half a letter grade and might mean the difference between a C+ and a B.

Whether several attributional retraining sessions are better than one session alone has been investigated in two studies (Menec and others, 1994, experiments 1 and 2). Students in a one-session condition viewed only one retraining videotape, whereas those in a two-session condition saw two different videotapes, one week apart. Although the two videotapes focused on different topics, one on failure in an academic achievement context and the second on failure in a sports context, both highlighted effort and study skills attributions. The findings are consistent across the two studies: one retraining session enhanced students' performance on a test; so did two sessions, but not more so than one session. One interpretation of these results is that viewing one videotape provided some novel information and therefore caused students to think about their own beliefs and perceptions. The second videotape, on the other hand, simply reiterated what had already been said, and as a result students' attributions did not change any further.

To date, nobody has examined whether multiple sessions provided by an attributional retrainer, rather than a videotape, would benefit college students. This approach might be particularly beneficial for students who have been disadvantaged all their lives, as in the case of certain ethnic minority groups or the physically disabled. These individuals are particularly prone to feelings of helplessness: believing they lack control over their environment, having low self-esteem, and the tendency to give up when faced with challenges. For these students, an intensive one-to-one attributional retraining intervention may be the only way to modify attributions.

*Attributional Retraining Benefits At-Risk Students.* The previous discussion might leave the reader with the impression that attributional retraining is universally effective. That is not the case. Attributional retraining benefits primarily students who are at risk academically. The definition of *at-risk* varies, but researchers generally have focused on such factors as a history of poor performance on tests in a course (Van Overwalle, Segebarth, and Goldchstein, 1989), an external locus of control, whereby individuals believe that they have little control over their environment (Menec and others, 1994, experiment 2, Perry and Penner, 1990), or a low GPA associated with worrying about the GPA (Wilson and Linville, 1982, 1985). To this list of risk factors could be added characteristics such as low self-esteem, low socioeconomic status, gender, and so on.

Some researchers included only at-risk students in their study. This decision was presumably based on the assumption that only these students would benefit from retraining. Other studies included both high-risk and low-risk students (Menec and others, 1994; Perry and Penner, 1990; Perry, Struthers, Menec, and Weinberg, 1994). The results are consistent across all these studies: attributional retraining enhances the performance of high-risk students—for example, those with an external locus of control—but has no effect on low-risk students, such as internal-locus students. This finding holds not only in laboratory experiments but also in field studies in which we investigated the effect of attributional retraining on actual course performance (Perry, Struthers, Menec, and Weinberg, 1994).

An issue that has not been examined systematically is whether attributional retraining is of benefit across disciplines. Some evidence that this is the case comes from research by Perry, Struthers, Menec, and Weinberg (1994) and Van Overwalle and De Metsenaere (1990), who found that attributional retraining enhanced students' performance in a psychology and an economics course, respectively. While attributional retraining should therefore be effective across disciplines, the critical issue is that some students are particularly at risk in certain disciplines. It is these high-risk individuals, such as female or minority students in the sciences and engineering, who should be targeted as candidates for attributional retraining. These interventions might be introduced to all students as part of an orientation session at the beginning of the academic year, for example. A more personal, and likely more effective, approach for high-risk students is to provide attributional retraining repeatedly over the year, perhaps as part of a mentoring or "buddy" system. Furthermore, attributional retraining should be of benefit when incorporated in a less structured fashion into regular classroom teaching.

## Implications for Teaching

Professors have to deal with a wide range of students. Some are highly motivated and will succeed regardless of the subject matter, teaching effectiveness, or class size. However, in every class there are likely to be several students who are at risk, because of lack of motivation, poor self-esteem, or a low sense of personal control. It is these students that faculty can help. We propose two implications that the research on attributions and attributional retraining has for faculty: (1) professors can function as attributional retrainers when interacting with students, and (2) professors should be aware of how their comments regarding students' performances and abilities may be interpreted by students.

**Be an Attributional Retrainer.** Although instructors probably lack the time or means to apply attributional retraining in a formal way in their courses, they can try to incorporate the principles of this technique informally. Adaptive attributions can be highlighted and modeled to the whole class, such as prior to a test or when returning tests or assignments. This informal type of attributional retraining should be particularly useful in disciplines that are stereotypically linked to innate ability.

For example, a calculus professor who is aware that mathematical skills are often attributed to ability (or lack thereof) can stress the importance of effort and persistence in how well students perform in the course. Faculty may want to tell students directly that effort is important and may provide suggestions as to how much time students should spend studying for the course. Similarly, a professor can give examples of effective ways to study the material, such as studying in groups. Faculty may even want to take it upon themselves to assign students to study groups.

The importance of effort and persistence can also be transmitted more indirectly. Anecdotal evidence of the experiences and struggles of important figures in a discipline can help students understand that these individuals did not become experts simply because of innate ability. A professor's personal experiences in becoming proficient in a domain may also prove valuable to students.

Faculty can also serve as attributional retrainers when talking to students on a one-to-one basis after class or during office hours. For example, talking with a student about performance on a test provides the professor with an excellent opportunity to explore the student's attributions. At this point, maladaptive attributions such as "I'm no good at this" or "The test was too difficult" can be countered with comments on the order of "Let's talk about how you prepared for the test" or "Test material appears easier when one studies effectively."

**Be Aware of How Students Might Interpret Your Comments.** Instructors use a variety of methods to motivate their students or put them at ease. Unfortunately, some of these strategies can have effects that are opposite to those intended. Consider one example that was related to us regarding a professor who frequently commented in class: "Any idiot could understand this." A charitable interpretation of this statement is that the instructor intended to convey that the material was quite easy, so easy in fact that even an idiot could learn it. But how would a student who does *not* understand the material interpret this statement? The implication seems to be "I must be even more stupid than an idiot," or "I'll look really stupid if I ask the prof to explain this." Either way, the consequences of this comment are detrimental, particularly for students who lack self-confidence, because it causes them to doubt their abilities and effectively prevents them from asking questions.

While the above example is undoubtedly an extreme one, a milder version might be a professor's saying, "Now this is very easy to understand." For the at-risk student who questions his or her ability to succeed in a particular course, this apparently innocuous comment may be equally devastating. Just as professors' comments can have negative consequences for students' motivation and achievement, they can also assist students. The statement "You all have the ability to do well in this course" not only motivates low-risk students, but it also benefits those who doubt their abilities. Thus faculty are well advised to carefully examine the methods they use to motivate students and ask themselves what consequences the methods might have for at-risk students. Similarly, they should be sensitive to any comments that may cast doubt on students' abilities, even inadvertently.

In sum, the present chapter focuses on attributional retraining as a method to enhance students' motivation and academic achievement. We have argued that some disciplines place certain students at risk because they are linked with "ability" myths. Attributional retraining can assist students who are at risk in such disciplines, as in the case of female students in mathematics and engineering. The critical aspect of attributional retraining is that students need to believe that their performance is modifiable and under their control. While the uniformly successful student is already aware of this, it is the at-risk student who needs to be convinced of her or his ability to succeed and who will benefit from professors' attributional retraining.

## References

Abramson, L. Y., Seligman, M.E.P., and Teasdale, J. "Learned Helplessness in Humans: Critique and Reformulation." *Journal of Personality and Social Psychology*, 1978, 87, 32–48.

Diener, C. I., and Dweck, C. S. "An Analysis of Learned Helplessness: Continuous Changes in Performance, Strategy, and Achievement Cognitions Following Failure." *Journal of Personality and Social Psychology*, 1978, 36, 451–462.

Fox, L., Brody, L., and Tobin, D. *Women and the Mathematical Mystique.* Baltimore: Johns Hopkins University Press, 1980.

Menec, V. H., Perry, R. P., Struthers, C. W., Schonwetter, D. J., Hechter, F. J., and Eichholz, B. L. "Assisting At-Risk College Students with Attributional Retraining and Effective Teaching." *Journal of Applied Social Psychology*, 1994, 24, 675–701.

Perry, R. P., Hechter, F. J., Menec, V. H., and Weinberg, L. "Enhancing Achievement Motivation and Performance in College Students: An Attributional Retraining Perspective." *Research in Higher Education*, 1993, 34, 687–723.

Perry, R. P., and Penner, K. P. "Enhancing Academic Achievement in College Students Through Attributional Retraining and Instruction." *Journal of Educational Psychology*, 1990, 82, 262–271.

Perry, R. P., Struthers, C. W., Menec, V. H., and Weinberg, L. *Attributional Retraining in the College Classroom: Some Cause(s) for Optimism.* Unpublished manuscript, University of Manitoba, Canada, 1994.

Van Overwalle, F., and De Metsenaere, M. "The Effect of Attribution-Based Intervention and Study Strategy Training on Academic Achievement in College Freshmen." *British Journal of Educational Psychology*, 1990, 60, 299–311.

Van Overwalle, F., Segebarth, K., and Goldchstein, M. "Improving Performance of Freshmen Through Attributional Testimonies from Fellow Students." *British Journal of Educational Psychology*, 1989, 59, 75–85.

Weiner, B. *An Attributional Theory of Motivation and Emotion.* New York: Springer, 1986.

Wilson, T. D., and Linville, P. W. "Improving the Academic Performance of College Freshmen: Attribution Therapy Revisited." *Journal of Personality and Social Psychology*, 1982, 42, 367–376.

Wilson, T. D., and Linville, P. W. "Improving the Performance of College Freshmen with Attributional Techniques." *Journal of Personality and Social Psychology*, 1985, 49, 287–293.

*Verena H. Menec is a postdoctoral fellow at the University of Manitoba.*

*Raymond P. Perry is a social psychologist who serves on the boards of four journals in the education field and recently edited a special edition of the* Journal of Educational Psychology *(1990) on college teaching.*

# Concluding Remarks: On the Meaning of Disciplinary Differences

*Michele Marincovich*

Building on the pioneering studies of Biglan (1973a, 1973b) and the more recent but already highly influential work of Shulman (1986, 1987, 1989), we set out to examine the role of disciplinary differences in three broad areas of postsecondary education: the organization of knowledge; the beliefs, attitudes, and perceptions of faculty; and the attitudes, strategies, and perceptions of students. The key question now is whether the research on disciplinary differences summarized in the previous eleven chapters brings us any closer to the goal of more effective teaching and learning in higher education.

## Two Lines of Argument

The answer from these chapters is yes, but through two very different, if implicit, lines of argument. One group of our authors assumes that we need to understand more fully the different educational worlds that faculty of different disciplinary groups (and of different institutional types, as Smart and Ethington remind us) inhabit. Only if we understand faculty's discipline-specific worlds can administrators, faculty developers, and peers help the faculty in each disciplinary group develop the teaching methods that are most effective for the nature of their content and their particular instructional goals for students. Professors' teaching will improve, as will student learning.

A second line of argument among our authors, again implicit, seeks to use knowledge of disciplinary differences to change the nature of teaching and learning in higher education and not simply to better match teaching methods to instructional goals. Although these authors are interested in and elucidate the nature of disciplinary differences, they identify important changes that higher education needs to undergo—regardless of discipline—in order to make faculty's teaching more fully effective for students and in order to maximize students' chances of successful learning.

## Understanding Different Disciplinary Worlds

Let us begin with the first line of argument and the chapters of Donald, Hativa, Cashin and Downey, Braxton, and Smart and Ethington.

Donald shows us that disciplinary differences among faculty begin with the very structure of knowledge in the university setting. Disciplines differ in the models that they use in their search to uncover and validate new knowledge; they even vary in the degree to which they deserve to be considered full-fledged disciplines. Those areas of knowledge, such as education and engineering, that are open-ended in their content and methodology are more properly called fields of study. As it turns out, however, in actual practice faculty of different disciplines show more agreement across disciplines and less agreement within their discipline on approaches to validation processes than theory would have it. Not surprisingly, given this lack of clarity on validation processes, faculty do not give clear instruction to their students on the creation and validation of knowledge.

Hativa takes this work on knowledge structures a step further by very intensively examining what kind of knowledge faculty are actually emphasizing in their lectures, and contrasting the teaching content of a faculty member in a pure field (physics) with that of a faculty member in an applied field (engineering). Like Donald (1983), Hativa finds that both professors are using a very large number of specialized concepts, but she also concludes that the member of the pure field expects students to learn to verify processes for themselves, while the professor in the applied field wants to make very sure that students can use processes (largely borrowed from physics) properly in practical ways. For the professor in the pure field, application means using theoretical concepts to predict experimental results; for the professor in the applied area, it means using abstract theories (while accepting that they are correct) to design useful devices.

At the macro level, working with data on thousands of faculty from the IDEA student evaluation system, Cashin and Downey hope to identify why faculty in the humanities and arts generally get higher student ratings than faculty in the social sciences, while faculty in the social sciences tend to do better than professors in math, engineering, and the sciences. They are unable to find out why, at least by analyzing the ratings of disciplines according to Biglan's scheme. They are able to conclude, however, that students reported more learning on the course objectives that faculty of a specific discipline had reported as more important (and thus, one assumes, had presumably emphasized in their teaching). Cashin and Downey further conclude that instructors received higher ratings from students on the teaching methods most relevant to the most important course objectives of that faculty member's discipline. Interestingly, however, their data also show that although a faculty member who wants to emphasize the learning of factual knowledge in her class may use more teaching methods related to that goal than to any other, she does not necessarily use more of these teaching methods than a faculty member who is not even trying to emphasize factual knowledge! In other words, even though professors of mathematics and statistics say that they weight the teaching of factual knowledge more heavily than professors in English or education say they do, students in the IDEA system do not find mathematicians and statisticians using more teaching methods appropriate for conveying factual knowledge than do their English and education professors.

Braxton along with Smart and Ethington round out our first group of authors. Braxton argues that faculty in the soft disciplines show more of an interest in students, student development issues, and general undergraduate education than faculty in the hard disciplines and thus are natural allies (in "affinity disciplines") for those who would seek to reform undergraduate education. Smart and Ethington suggest that we stop debating goals for undergraduate education altogether and instead concentrate on assisting faculty to improve their instructional effectiveness in reaching the goals appropriate to their discipline and the nature of their content. They probably make the strongest argument for the fact that knowledge of disciplinary differences should help us to facilitate faculty's attainment of the goals associated with their disciplinary cluster. To do this effectively, they urge, we would do well to follow the example of researchers on primary and secondary teaching and do more discipline-specific pedagogical research that goes beyond "low-inference" behaviors.

## Using Knowledge of Differences to Create Change

The second line of argument, using knowledge of disciplinary differences to change the nature of teaching and learning in higher education and not simply to better match teaching methods to instructional goals, implicitly emerges in the chapters of Murray and Renaud, Franklin and Theall, Stodolsky and Grossman, Menec and Perry, Entwhistle and Tait, and Lenze. Murray and Renaud suggest, for example, that the reason faculty in the sciences receive lower ratings from students than those in the humanities and social sciences is that science professors display fewer of the low-inference teaching behaviors that are associated with good teaching. Faculty in the sciences and engineering should be encouraged to use more of these behaviors, especially in the rapport and interaction categories. Franklin and Theall are also concerned with what it is that influences student ratings of instructors. They suggest we look for correlates, such as the time-valued ratio recently suggested by Gillmore's research (1994), that allow us to examine factors crucial to effective teaching. In the meantime, they urge professors (and the faculty developers who work with them) to scrutinize the value of the course assignments and materials that they give to students in order to increase the time-valued ratio. They also exhort researchers on student evaluation to try to construct rating forms that capture not only students' in-class experiences with teaching but also the impact of the overall course design and implementation.

Stodolsky and Grossman, although focusing on the role of disciplines in secondary education, suggest that there is a "hidden curriculum," a subtext, in the organization of study in higher education. This hidden curriculum powerfully influences students', and therefore future secondary teachers', perceptions of how high school classes should be organized and whether students' own abilities or the nature of the field will determine their success. Menec and Perry would agree that there is this hidden curriculum in higher education, although they call it the "myths" that are associated with certain disciplines in higher education. For some students, exposure to these myths may confirm their own doubts about their abilities to succeed in disciplines where it is assumed that innate ability is the overriding determinant of success. Menec and Perry believe that faculty can minimize the myths for the most vulnerable students, those who are at risk, by becoming attributional retrainers of their students. By their comments in class and in office-hours interactions with students, faculty can stress the role of hard work and dedication, rather than sheer ability, in succeeding at their courses.

Entwistle and Tait challenge faculty to advance the learning of all students by incorporating into each discipline, through specialized courseware, assignments and exercises that will help students to learn about learning in that field. Faculty should not look to study-skill specialists to work with students whose study strategies are not successful; instead, for the sake of their students, disciplinary specialists should also become specialists on the learning of their discipline. In this process faculty need to become aware of how their own teaching approaches, especially the types of tests they give, influence students' study strategies. Although faculty may assume that students too easily succumb to cramming and shallow learning, certain disciplines seem to do a better job than others of encouraging students to learn deeply.

In her studies of new faculty, Lenze too believes (following Grossman's lead in her study [1990]) that "knowledge of students' understandings" is a major component of the overall knowledge of teaching that novice faculty must develop. There are three other critical areas: the reasons for teaching a certain discipline, appropriate instructional strategies, and knowledge of the curriculum in which one's course is embedded. Lenze believes, however, that underlying all these components, each discipline has an often unspoken but essential core aspect—a conceptual approach around which all teaching endeavors are organized. Although new teachers themselves may not be conscious of or see the importance of their discipline's core concept (again, the hidden curriculum), they will benefit from hearing the concept reflected back to them and discussing it. Although Lenze does not mention arguing with or trying to change a discipline's core concept, her notion of making the concept tacit opens it to examination and perhaps transformation.

## To Support or to Transform?

Does one of these two lines of implicit argument between our authors win out? Where will knowledge of disciplinary differences make more of a contribution to the quality of higher education: if this knowledge is used to better understand and therefore better support faculty's already existing instructional goals, or if the knowledge is used to better understand and transform these goals?

First, the knowledge itself of disciplinary differences is still growing and is still a thin, though uplifting, reed for either support or transformation of higher education. For example, although Donald has laid a foundation for understanding disciplinary differences in knowledge validation processes, much more work needs to be done on how, and to what extent, faculty teach these processes to their students and what contribution this knowledge makes to students' understanding of the discipline. Hativa's promising and close examination of individual lectures needs to be applied now to lectures in hard versus soft fields and (though the payoff here will likely be much less) to life versus nonlife disciplines. Although we have tantalizing clues and plausible explanations for the systematic variations in student ratings of faculty from various disciplinary groups (Murray and Renaud, Franklin and Theall, and Cashin and Downey), we need to do more work to pin down these causes. Until we do, we must continue to be very cautious about—if not prohibited from—using the results of student evaluations to make comparisons across disciplines.

In the whole area of student learning, the examination of disciplinary differences is especially new. Entwistle and Tait and Menec and Perry have rather courageously opened up the research on student learning to disciplinary differences and have had to venture even further than most of our other authors from established studies and approaches.

Second, we have not even begun to tap for comparative purposes the experiences and data of those faculty and students who deliberately cross disciplinary lines. How do students evaluate the classes of faculty whose courses do not fit cleanly into Biglan's cells? What are the learning experiences and problems of students who create their own interdisciplinary majors? How do the teaching goals of interdisciplinary faculty compare to those of their disciplinary colleagues? Would reports from this group of faculty and students make our data muddier or clearer? Would research from the secondary level on the approaches of science teachers trained in physics versus science teachers trained in biology speak to the experiences of university-level physicists and biologists who collaborate to teach an interdisciplinary science course?

## Common Ground

As the research base on disciplinary differences builds up and grows to embrace interdisciplinary faculty and students, perhaps we will see this work as not leading to a forced choice between supporting faculty's existing goals or transforming them. Knowledge of disciplinary differences may itself mute the parochialism and shortsightedness that often accompany those differences. We may find, as Donald did, that when we talk to faculty more about their actual experience of disciplinary differences, there is common ground. As such different approaches to better teaching as peer teaching evaluation, technology in teaching, and assessment techniques all focus more attention on student learning, faculty of all disciplines may find themselves to be working the most important common ground of all.

## References

Biglan, A. "The Characteristics of Subject Matter in Different Academic Areas." *Journal of Applied Psychology,* 1973a, *57* (3), 195–203.

Biglan, A. "Relationships Between Subject Matter Characteristics and the Structure and Output of University Departments." *Journal of Applied Psychology,* 1973b, *57* (3), 204–213.

Donald, J. G. "Knowledge Structures: Methods for Exploring Course Content." *Journal of Higher Education,* 1983, *54,* 31–41.

Gillmore, G. "The Effects of Course Demands and Grading Leniency on Student Ratings of Instruction." Paper presented at the annual meeting of the American Educational Research Association, Atlanta, April 1994.

Grossman, P. L. *The Making of a Teacher: Teacher Knowledge and Teacher Education.* New York: Teachers College Press, 1990.

Shulman, L. S. "Those Who Understand: Knowledge Growth in Teaching." *Educational Researcher,* 1986, *15,* 4–14.

Shulman, L. S. "Knowledge and Teaching: Foundations of the New Reform." *Harvard Educational Review,* 1987, *57,* 1–22.

Shulman, L. S. "Toward a Pedagogy of Substance." *AAHE Bulletin,* June 1989, 8–13.

*Michele Marincovich is director of the Center for Teaching and Learning at Stanford University.*

# INDEX

Abramson, L. Y., 105
Academic success: attributional retraining and, 105; causal attributions and, 106–106; disciplinary differences and, 93, 105–110; innate ability and, 105; stereotypes about, 105; studying and, 105
Administrators, disciplinary implications for, 62–63
Affinity disciplines: academic affairs administrators and, 62–63; educational reform and, 61; faculty development and, 62; program review and, 62; soft disciplines as, 61; student-centered nature of, 61
Assessment. *See* Student assessment; Student ratings
Association of American Colleges (AAC), 49
Atkinson, J., 75
Attributional retraining: at-risk students and, 109–110; causal attributions and, 106–107; cross-discipline, 110; defined, 105, 107; discussion-focused, 108–109; effectiveness of, 107; GPA and, 107–108; methods, 108–110; session length/number, 108–109; studies of, 107–108; teacher comments and, 111–112; teaching implications and, 110–112; theoretical basis of, 105; video-taped, 108–109
Avery, R. W., 10, 14

Bain, J. D., 101
Barnes, J., 65
Barnes, L.L.B., 82
Barnes, M. W., 82
Becher, T., 7, 65
Bentley, R. J., 60
Beynon, C., 65
Biggs, J. B., 94, 101
Biglan, A., 1, 8, 10, 19, 32, 50, 59, 76, 82, 113
Bloom, B. S., 83
Boyer, E. L., 61
Brackett, G. C., 9
Braxton, J. M., 59, 60, 61
Brody, L., 107

Broudy, H. S., 9
Brownell, J., 7

Calder, I., 100
Carnegie Foundation for the Advancement of Teaching, 50
Cashin, W. E., 32, 34, 42, 81, 82, 83, 88, 90
Centra, J. A., 31
Chickering, A. W., 62
Clark, C. M., 65
Clegg, V. L., 81
Cohen, D. K., 77
Cohen, P. A., 46, 83
Coherence, 14–15
Concepts: defined, 20; disciplinary differences and, 20; engineering vs. physics instruction (study), 19–26; as level of knowledge, 20; purpose of, 20
Conflicting evidence, 12–13, 15
Consistency, 10, 13, 15
Cranton, P. A., 82
Critical thinking, 8–9, 15, 90
Curriculum: English, 75; faculty pedagogical content knowledge of, 67–68; hidden, 77; mathematics, 74–75; secondary school teachers and, 74–76
Cushman, H. R., 55

De Metsenaere, M., 108, 110
Diener, C. I., 106
Disciplinary differences: academic success and, 93, 105–110; Association of American Colleges task forces and, 49; attributions and, 106–107; Biglan's model of, 1, 7–8, 10, 19, 32, 50, 59–60, 82; concepts and, 20; creating change and, 115–116; forms of understanding and, 98–99; future directions in, 117; how students are taught and, 89–90; institutional mission and, 50; instructional consultants and, 1; instructional differences and, 31–32; instructional goals and, 31; knowledge types and, 19; knowledge validation process and, 8–10; learning environment and, 99–101; learning styles and, 94; need for studies on, 2; paradigmatic development framework

# ORDERING INFORMATION

NEW DIRECTIONS FOR TEACHING AND LEARNING is a series of paperback books that presents ideas and techniques for improving college teaching, based both on the practical expertise of seasoned instructors and on the latest research findings of educational and psychological researchers. Books in the series are published quarterly in spring, summer, fall, and winter and are available for purchase by subscription as well as by single copy.

SUBSCRIPTIONS for 1995 cost $48.00 for individuals (a savings of 25 percent over single-copy prices) and $64.00 for institutions, agencies, and libraries. Please do not send institutional checks for personal subscriptions. Standing orders are accepted. (For subscriptions outside of North America, add $7.00 for shipping via surface mail or $25.00 for air mail. Orders *must be prepaid* in U.S. dollars by check drawn on a U.S. bank or charged to VISA, MasterCard, or American Express.)

SINGLE COPIES cost $16.95 plus shipping (see below) when payment accompanies order. California, New Jersey, New York, and Washington, D.C., residents please include appropriate sales tax. Canadian residents add GST and any local taxes. Billed orders will be charged shipping and handling. No billed shipments to post office boxes. (Orders from outside North America *must be prepaid* in U.S. dollars by check drawn on a U.S. bank or charged to VISA, MasterCard, or American Express.)

SHIPPING (SINGLE COPIES ONLY): $10.00 and under, add $2.50; to $20.00, add $3.50; to $50.00, add $4.50; to $75.00, add $5.50; to $100.00, add $6.50; to $150.00, add $7.50; over $150.00, add $8.50.

DISCOUNTS FOR QUANTITY ORDERS are available. Please write to the address below for information.

ALL ORDERS must include either the name of an individual or an official purchase order number. Please submit your order as follows:
   *Subscriptions:* specify series and year subscription is to begin
   *Single copies:* include individual title code (such as TL54)

MAIL ALL ORDERS TO:
   Jossey-Bass Publishers
   350 Sansome Street
   San Francisco, CA 94104-1342

FOR SUBSCRIPTION SALES OUTSIDE OF THE UNITED STATES, CONTACT:
   any international subscription agency or Jossey-Bass directly.